AUTOCAD® 2010
ESSENTIALS

Munir M. Hamad

Autodesk® Approved Instructor

JONES AND BARTLETT PUBLISHERS

Sudbury, Massachusetts

BOSTON   TORONTO   LONDON   SINGAPORE

World Headquarters

Jones and Bartlett Publishers
40 Tall Pine Drive
Sudbury, MA 01776
978-443-5000
info@jbpub.com
www.jbpub.com

Jones and Bartlett Publishers
Canada
6339 Ormindale Way
Mississauga, Ontario L5V 1J2
Canada

Jones and Bartlett Publishers
International
Barb House, Barb Mews
London W6 7PA
United Kingdom

Jones and Bartlett's books and products are available through most bookstores and online booksellers. To contact Jones and Bartlett Publishers directly, call 800-832-0034, fax 978-443-8000, or visit our website www.jbpub.com.

Substantial discounts on bulk quantities of Jones and Bartlett's publications are available to corporations, professional associations, and other qualified organizations. For details and specific discount information, contact the special sales department at Jones and Bartlett via the above contact information or send an email to specialsales@jbpub.com.

Autodesk, AutoCAD are registered trademarks or trademarks of Autodesk, Inc., and/or its subsidiaries and/or affiliates in the USA and/or other countries. All other brand names, product names, or trademarks belong to their respective holders. Autodesk reserves the right to alter product offerings and specifications at any time without notice, and is not responsible for typographical or graphical errors that may appear in this document. © 2010 Autodesk, Inc. All rights reserved.

AutoCAD® 2010 design and documentation software, one of the world's leading CAD programs, allows you to speed up documentation, share ideas accurately, and explore ideas more intuitively in 3D. It is powerful and flexible, and you can customize it for your specific needs.

Production Credits

Publisher: David Pallai
Editorial Assistant: Melissa Potter
Production Director: Amy Rose
Production Manager: Jennifer Bagdigian
Associate Production Editor: Melissa Elmore
Senior Marketing Manager:
 Andrea DeFronzo

V.P., Manufacturing and Inventory Control:
 Therese Connell
Composition: International Typesetting
 and Composition, Inc.
Cover Design: Kristin E. Parker
Cover Image: © Happy Alex/ShutterStock, Inc.
Printing and Binding: Malloy, Inc.
Cover Printing: Malloy, Inc.

Library of Congress Cataloging-in-Publication Data
Hamad, Munir M.
 AutoCAD 2010 essentials / Munir Hamad.
  p. cm.
 Includes bibliographical references.
 ISBN 978-0-7637-7629-9 (pbk.)
 1. Computer graphics. 2. Computer-aided design. 3. AutoCAD. I. Title.
 T385.H32933 2009
 620'.00420285536--dc22

                                      2009010994
6048
Printed in the United States of America
13 12 11 10 09   10 9 8 7 6 5 4 3 2 1

TABLE OF CONTENTS

PREFACE

◊   AutoCAD® has been the de facto drafting tool for PC users since 1982. As you read this, millions and millions of engineers, draftsmen, project managers, and engineering students are creating their drawings with AutoCAD.

◊   This book is perfect for new and novice users of AutoCAD 2010. It is also a very handy tool for college and university drafting instructors using AutoCAD 2010.

◊   This book will not teach what engineering drafting is or how to produce it. Knowing drafting and design concepts are prerequisites for using this book.

◊   This text can be instructor-led or self-taught.

  •   The estimated time to complete instructor-led courseware is three days at eight hours a day.

  •   If you opt to teach yourself, you have the luxury of completing the courseware at your own pace.

◊   At the end of each chapter, you will find Chapter Review questions that will help you test yourself to see if you understand the subject.

◊   There are 40 exercises integrated throughout the book to help you quickly implement what you have learned.

◊   There are 21 workshops that, together, will complete a full project (a small villa), starting with the creation of the project through plotting. Solving all of the workshops will teach you to:

  •   Simulate a real-life project from beginning to end, thereby allowing you to implement what you have learned.

• Organize the information in a logical order.

• Learn all of the basic commands and functions in AutoCAD 2010.

◊ This text will cover the basic and intermediate levels of AutoCAD 2010.

PURPOSE AND OBJECTIVES

◊ At the completion of this book, the reader will be able to:

• Understand what AutoCAD is and how to deal with its basic operations, including the filing system

• Draw different objects with speed and precision

• Set up drawings

• Construct drawings in simple steps

• Modify any object in a drawing

• Create, insert, and edit blocks

• Hatch using different hatch patterns and methods

• Create text and tables

• Insert and edit dimensions

• Prepare and plot a drawing

PREREQUISITES

◊ The author assumes that you have experience using computers and the Microsoft® Windows® operating system.

◊ Also, you should have knowledge of starting new files, opening existing files, saving files, using "Save As" with files, closing files with or without saving, and exiting software.

◊ Because these commands are similar in all software packages, the author does not cover these subjects, unless it is necessary to demonstrate a command specific to AutoCAD.

ABOUT THE DVD

◊   A DVD is included in the book and contains the following:

- The AutoCAD 2010 trial version, which will last for 30 days starting from the day of installation. This version will help you solve all of the exercises and workshops in the book. Students with a valid university email address can visit http://students8.autodesk.com/?lbon=1 for student versions of the AutoCAD material for the duration of the class.

- Exercise and workshop files, which will be your starting point to solving all exercises and workshops in the book. Copy the **Book Exercises** and **Book Workshops** folder onto your hard drive. You will find two folders inside the workshop folder. The first one is named **Metric** for the metric units workshops, and the second one is named **Imperial** for the imperial units workshops.

Chapter **1**

INTRODUCTION TO AUTOCAD® 2010

1.1 WHAT IS AUTOCAD®?

- AutoCAD® was one of the first Computer Aided Design/Drafting (CAD) software applications in the world.
- The first version of AutoCAD was released at the end of 1982, and it was designed to be used only on PCs.
- Since 1982, AutoCAD has increased dramatically on a global scale.
- Users can draw both two-dimensional (2D) drawings and three-dimensional (3D) designs in AutoCAD.
- There is another version of AutoCAD called AutoCAD LT that is dedicated to 2D drafting only.

1.2 HOW TO START AUTOCAD® 2010

AutoCAD 2010
- English

- There are two ways to start AutoCAD 2010:
  - While installing AutoCAD 2010, the installation program will create a shortcut on your desktop. To start AutoCAD, simply double-click this icon.
  - From the **Windows** taskbar click **Start/All Programs/Autodesk/ AutoCAD2010/AutoCAD2010**.
- AutoCAD will start with a new, open drawing file, which will look like the following:

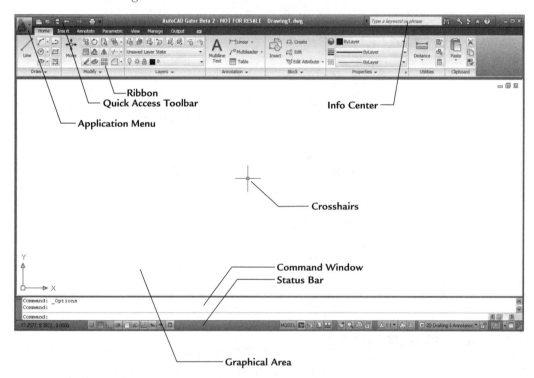

1.3 UNDERSTANDING THE AUTOCAD® 2010 INTERFACE

- The primary methods to reach commands in AutoCAD 2010 will be through **Ribbons** and the **Application Menu**.
- You will use **Ribbons** instead of the normal toolbars.
- This interface will give you more space in the **Graphical Area**, which is your drawing area.

Application Menu

- Click on the **Application Menu**, and you will see the following:

- Using this menu, you can:
  - Create a new file
  - Open an existing file
  - Save the current file
  - Save the current file under a new name (Save As) and/or in a different folder
  - Export the current file to a different file format
  - Print the current file
  - Publish the current file
  - Send the current file to eTransmit or email
  - Use all the functions related to your drawing

- Close the current file
- Exit AutoCAD

Quick Access Toolbar

- The **Quick Access Toolbar** is the small toolbar located at the top left of the screen:

- Using this toolbar, you can:
  - Create a new file
  - Open an existing file
  - Save the current file
  - Undo and redo
  - Print the current file

Ribbons

- **Ribbons** consist of two parts:
  - Tabs
  - Panels
- For example, the **Home** tab consists of eight panels: **Draw**, **Modify**, **Layers**, **Annotation**, **Block**, **Properties**, **Utilities**, and **Clipboard**.
- In each tab you will see different panels.
- The following is the **Draw** panel:

- Some panels (such as the **Draw** panel) have a small triangle near the title, which indicates that there are more buttons available. If you click on it you will see the following:

- At the lower left-hand corner of the panel you will see a small pushpin. If you click on it, this will be the default view. To return to the previous view, simply click the pushpin again.

- Some panel buttons may have a small triangle just to the right, which means there are additional options, as shown here:

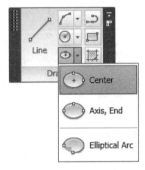

- If you hold your cursor over any button for one second, a small help screen appears:

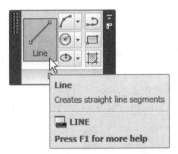

- However, if you hold your cursor over the button for three seconds, you will see an extended help screen:

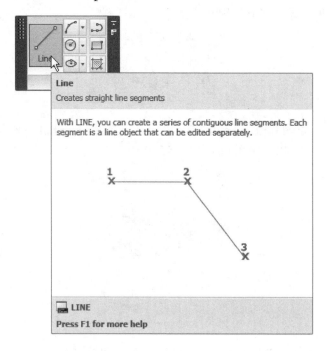

- Panels can be docked or floating. By default, all panels are docked. To make a panel a floating panel, simply click on the name of the panel, hold it, and drag it to its new location.
- If all panels remain docked, you will *not* see any panel outside the tab it belongs to. But if you make any panel a floating panel, then you will be able to see it in all other tabs.
- While the panel is floating, you will see two small buttons on the right-hand side. The following image shows the function of each one:

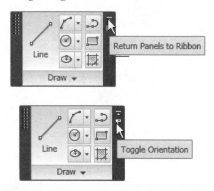

- All panels have two orientations: a vertical orientation and a horizontal orientation. The following illustration shows the tabs and panels that appear for both orientations.

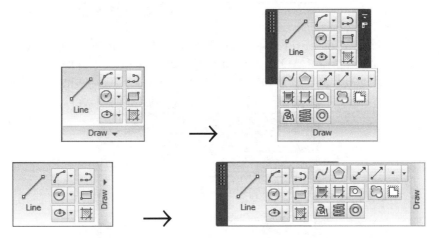

- The number of tabs and panels are predefined by default.
- You can turn off/on any tab/panel by right-clicking on any tab/panel and then selecting the desired tab/panel to be turned on or off.

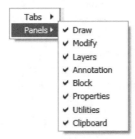

- **Ribbons** have three different shapes. You can alter the shapes by clicking the small arrow at the right:

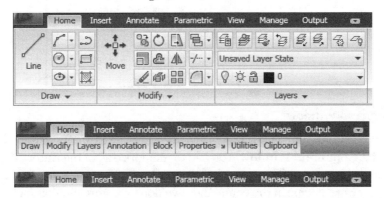

InfoCenter

- At the top-right part of the screen, you will see the **InfoCenter**:

- The **InfoCenter** gives you the opportunity to type in keywords that will enable AutoCAD to search both online and offline resources and provide you with a list of related help topics. See the following example:

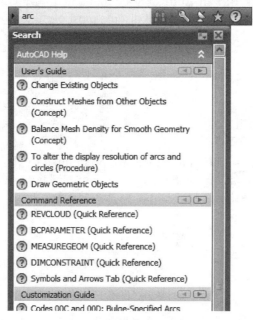

- You may still use the conventional **Help** search by clicking the arrow at the right-hand side of the **InfoCenter**:

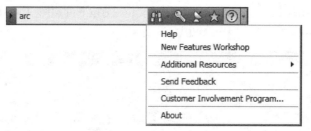

Command Window

- If you used AutoCAD 25 years ago, the only way to input commands was to use the **Command Window**. You had to memorize all of the AutoCAD commands and type them in. There were no **menus**, **toolbars**, **panels**, or **ribbons**. Although you can still type in the commands, we don't recommend that method.

Graphical Area

- The **Graphical Area** is where you do your actual drawing. You use the crosshairs to specify points in the X,Y plane.
- You can monitor the coordinates of the crosshairs using the left side of the **Status Bar**.

Status Bar

- The **Status Bar** in AutoCAD contains many functions that will help you draft more precisely. We will discuss most of the buttons on the **Status Bar** throughout this book.
- There are two views for the **Status Bar**:
  - By default (Icons)

  - Buttons

- To switch views, right-click the **Status Bar** to alternate between buttons and icons.

- If you select **Use Icons**, the view will change accordingly.

1.4 POINTS IN AUTOCAD®

- Points are defined (and saved) in AutoCAD using the **Cartesian coordinate system**.
- The coordinates will look something like **3.25,5.45**, which is the format of **X,Y**.
- So the first and most traditional way of specifying points in AutoCAD is to type the coordinates whenever you are asked to do so, by typing X,Y (pronounced X comma Y). See the following illustration:

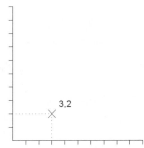

1.5 AUTOCAD® DEFAULT SETTINGS

- Sign convention: positive is up and right.
- Angle convention: positive is counterclockwise (CCW) starting from the east (i.e., 0 angle). See the following illustration:

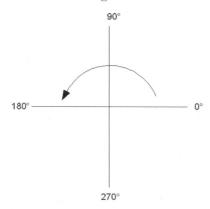

1.6 THINGS YOU SHOULD KNOW ABOUT AUTOCAD®

- The mouse is the primary input device:
  - The left mouse button is always used to select and/or click.
  - The right mouse button, when clicked, offers a drop-down menu.
- The mouse wheel has zooming functions:
  - Zoom in on your drawing by moving the wheel forward.
  - Zoom out of your drawing by moving the wheel backward.
  - Pan (i.e., move through the drawing) by pressing the wheel and holding it and then moving the mouse.
  - Zoom to the edges of your drawing by double-clicking the wheel.
- If you type an AutoCAD command or any input in the **Command Window**, you have to press the [Enter] key to execute it.
- [Enter] = [Spacebar] in AutoCAD.
- To repeat the last AutoCAD command, press [Enter] or [Spacebar].
- To cancel any AutoCAD command, press [Esc].

1.7 DRAWING LIMITS

- AutoCAD offers users an infinite drawing sheet on all sides.
- When you start a new AutoCAD drawing, your viewpoint will be at 0,0,1.
- You are looking at the X,Y plane, using a camera's lens; hence you will see part of your infinite drawing sheet. This part is called the **limits**. See the following:

- In this example, you can see that the **limits** of the drawing are from 0,0 (lower left-hand corner) to 12,9 (upper right-hand corner). This is your working area.
- We will learn how to change **limits** in upcoming chapters.

1.8 UNITS AND SPACES

- One of the vague facts about AutoCAD is that it does not deal with a certain length unit while drafting. Take note of the following points:
  - AutoCAD deals with AutoCAD units.
  - An AutoCAD unit can be anything you want. It can be a meter, centimeter, millimeter, inch, or foot.
  - All of these options are correct as long as you remember your chosen option and stay consistent in both X and Y.
- Also, there are two spaces in AutoCAD, **Model Space** and **Paper Space (Layout)**. You can switch between the two spaces using the **Status Bar**.

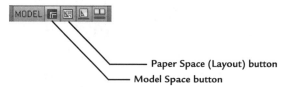

- By default, when you start a new drawing file, you are in **Model Space**.
- In **Model Space** you can create and modify your drawing.
- Once you are ready to make a hardcopy of your drawing file, switch to the **Paper Space (Layouts)** so you can prepare your page setup.
- This is the moment you need to ask, *"What is my unit assumption?"* so that you can properly scale your drawing.
- We will discuss printing in a later chapter.

1.9 VIEWING COMMANDS

- We already discussed using the mouse wheel for zooming in, zooming out, and panning.
- You can also zoom in, zoom out, and pan using the zooming and panning commands.
- If using **Ribbons**, make sure you are in the **View** tab, and, using the **Navigate** panel, select the first button on the left, or the small arrow, to see a list of zooming commands:

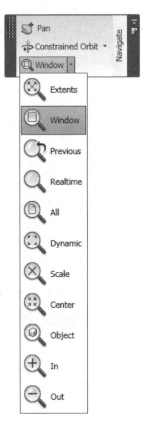

- **Zoom Extents** is used to zoom to all objects.
- **Zoom Window** is used to specify a rectangle. By specifying two opposite corners, whatever is inside the rectangle will look larger.
- **Zoom Previous** is used to restore the previous view, up to the last ten views.
- **Zoom Realtime** is done by clicking the left button on the mouse and holding it. If you move forward, you are zooming in; if you move backward, you are zooming out.
- **Zoom Dynamic** is used with the **Zoom Window** first. You will see the whole drawing and your current place (shown as a dotted green line), go to the new location, and press [Enter].
- **Zoom Scale** is used to input a scale factor. If you type in a number less than 1, you will see the drawing smaller. If the scale factor you type in is greater than 1, you will see the drawing larger. If you put the letter x after the number (e.g., 2x) the scale will be relative to the current view.
- **Zoom Center** is used to specify a new center point for the zooming, along with a new height.
- **Zoom Object** is used to zoom to certain selected objects. AutoCAD will ask you to select objects and the selected objects will fill the screen.
- **Zoom In** is not really a zoom option, but rather a programmed option equal to the **Zoom Scale** with a scale factor of 2x.
- **Zoom Out** is just like **Zoom In**, but with a zoom factor of 0.5x.

■ Also on the Status Bar, you can use the following two buttons:

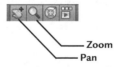

Zoom
Pan

1.10 CREATING A NEW FILE

■ To create a new file based on a premade template, click on the **New** button on the **Quick Access Toolbar**:

- The following dialog box will appear:

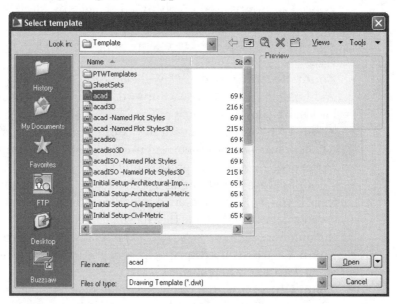

- This dialogue box will allow you to select the desired template.
- AutoCAD template files have the extension *.dwt*.
- AutoCAD 2010 has lots of premade templates you can use, or you can create your own template.
- For now, we will use *acad.dwt* for some of our exercises.
- Click **Open** to start a new file.

1.11 OPENING AN EXISTING FILE

- To open an existing file for further editing, click the **Open** button from the **Quick Access Toolbar**.

- The following dialog box will appear:

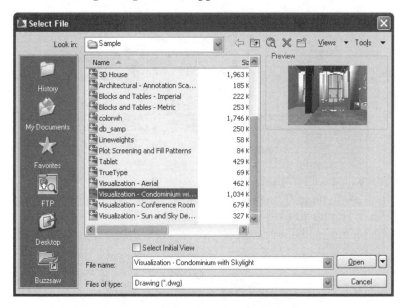

- Specify the hard drive, and the folder your file resides in.
- AutoCAD drawing files have the extension **.dwg*.
- If you want to open a single file, select the file and click open (you can also double-click on the file's name).
- If you want to open more than one file, select the first file name, then hold the [Ctrl] key on the keyboard, and click the other file names.
- You can open as many files as you wish.
- When you are done, click **Open**.

Quick View

- If you open more than one file, you can use two functions in the **Status Bar**: **Quick View Drawings** and **Quick View Layouts**.

Quick View Drawings
Quick View Layout

- If these two buttons are switched on, you will see the following:

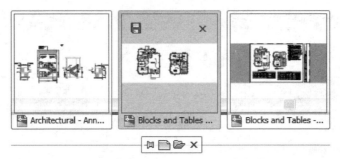

- You will see all of the open files.
- In order to jump from one file to another, click the window of the desired file.
- When you hover over any of the files, you will see the layouts of the file, and the picture will change to:

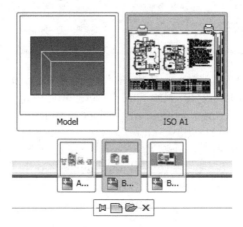

- Also, you will see a small toolbar at the bottom of the screen that will enable you to:
  - Close the **Quick View**
  - Open a file
  - Start a new file
  - Pin **Quick View Drawings**
- If you right-click the **Quick View** button of any file, the following menu will appear:

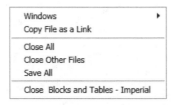

- You can close all files
- Close other files except the current file
- Save all files
- Close the current file

Organizing Files

- Make sure you are in the **View** tab on the **Ribbon**. There are several ways to organize the files by using the **Windows** panel.

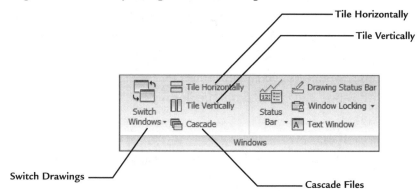

- The **Switch Drawings** button will show you a list of the opened files. The current file will be listed with a checkmark (✔). If you want another file, select the name of the desired file.

 - The rest of file commands, such as **Save**, **Save As**, and **Exit**, are identical to those in other Windows applications.

INTRODUCING AUTOCAD® 2010

 Exercise 1

1. Start AutoCAD 2010.
2. From the **Quick Access Toolbar**, click the **Open** button.
3. Go to the **Samples** folder under the AutoCAD 2010 folder. Open the following three files:
   a. Blocks and Tables—*Metric.dwg*
   b. *dbsamp.dwg*
   c. Architectural and Annotation Scaling—*Multileader.dwg*
4. Using **Quick View Drawings**, jump from one file to another. Using **Quick View Layouts**, take a look at the layouts in each file.
5. Using one of the open files, use the mouse wheel—like any of the other methods discussed in this chapter—and zoom in, zoom out, and pan.
6. Using the right-click menu on the **Quick View Drawings**, close all files without saving.

CHAPTER REVIEW

1. You can close all open files using one command:
    a. True
    b. False

2. CAD stands for_____.

3. In AutoCAD there are two available spaces: **Model Space** and **Paper Space**. Which of the following statements is true?
    a. You draw on **Model Space** and print from **Paper Space**.
    b. You draw in **Paper Space** and print from **Model Space**.
    c. There is only one space in AutoCAD.
    d. **Model Space** is only for 3D design.

4. Positive angles start from the north.
    a. True
    b. False

5. AutoCAD is one of the few software applications that allows users to:
    a. Connect to the Internet.
    b. Type commands using the keyboard.
    c. Accept Cartesian coordinates.
    d. Create positive angles that are CCW.

6. _____ is a tool in AutoCAD that allows users to see all open files in small windows.

CHAPTER REVIEW ANSWERS

1. a
2. Computer Aided Design/Drafting
3. a
4. b
5. b
6. **Quick View Drawings**

Chapter **2**

DRAFTING USING AUTOCAD® 2010

In This Chapter

2.1 INTRODUCTION

- The two most important things in drafting are:
  - Precision
  - Speed
- You always want to finish your drawing as fast as possible, yet you do not want to undermine your drawing's precision.
- It is best to learn precision before speed because it is easier to learn to speed up the creation process than it is to improve accuracy.
- In this chapter we will tackle many commands, but learning to draft with precision is most important.

2.2 THE LINE COMMAND

- The **Line** command is used to draw segments of straight lines.
- There are many methods available to draw precise shapes using the **Line** command (which we will learn later). For now, we will type coordinates in the **Command Window**.
- On the **Ribbon**, make sure you are in the **Home** tab. Using the **Draw** panel, click the **Line** button.

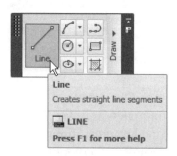

- The following prompts will appear:

```
Specify first point: (type in the coordinate of
the first point)
Specify next point or [Undo]: (type in the
coordinate of the second point)
Specify next point or [Undo]: (type in the
coordinate of the third point)
Specify next point or [Close/Undo]: (type in the
coordinate of the fourth point)
```

- You can use the **Undo** option at any time to undo the last specified point, hence the last specified segment.
- After you draw two segments, the **Close** option will be available to connect the last point to the first point and to end the command.
- Other ways of ending the command include pressing [Enter] or [Spacebar].
- You can also press [Esc] to end the **Line** command.
- If you are using the **Line** command and you right-click, you will get the following menu (which is identical to the command prompt):

2.3 DRAFTING USING DYNAMIC INPUT

- By default, the **Dynamic Input** is turned on, so anything you type in the **Command Window** will appear on the screen beside the AutoCAD® cursor.
- Make sure the **Dynamic Input** button is turned on:

- For example, if you type the word "line," here is how it will look on the screen:

- When you press [Enter], the following will appear:

- Type the X coordinates, then press the [Tab] key and you will see the following:

- Type the Y coordinates, then press [Enter] and **Dynamic Input** will show the length and the angle of the line to be drawn (the angle is measured from the east and incremented by 1 degree).

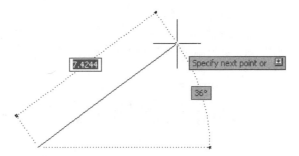

- Specify the length, press the [Tab] key, then type the angle and press [Enter]:

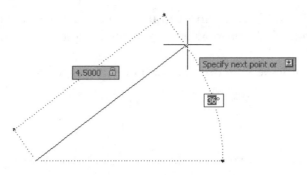

DRAWING LINES: FIRST METHOD

Exercise 2

1. Start AutoCAD 2010.
2. Open the file *Exercise_02.dwg*.
3. Make sure that **Polar Input** is off and **Dynamic Input** is on.
4. Draw the following lines using the **Line** command and **Dynamic Input**:

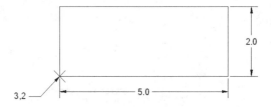

5. Save the file and close it.

- Start the **Line** command and then type the coordinates of the first point. While **Dynamic Input** is on, specify the length of the line, press [Tab], and then specify the angle. Do the same for the other line segments.

2.4 PRECISION METHOD 1: SNAP AND GRID

- As you can see, the only method we used to precisely specify points in the X,Y plane was to type the coordinates using **Dynamic Input**.
- We do this because we cannot depend on the mouse to specify precise points.
- In order to use the mouse precisely, we have to use tools to control its movement.
- **Snap** is the only tool in AutoCAD that can help us control the movement of the mouse.
- Using the **Status Bar**, click on the **Snap Mode** button.

- Now, move to the **Graphical Area** and watch the mouse jump to exact points.
- The **Grid** will show a grid of points on the screen similar to grid paper, which is used in drawing diagrams (these points are not real points).
- A **Grid** on its own is not accurate, but it is a helpful tool to use with **Snap**.
- On the **Status Bar**, click on the **Grid** button.

- You can now see the points displayed on the screen.
- If you think the default values for either **Snap** or **Grid** do not satisfy your needs, simply right-click one of the two buttons and the following shortcut menu will appear:

- Select **Settings** and the following dialog box will appear:

- By default, **Snap X spacing** and **Snap Y spacing** are equal; **Grid X spacing** and **Grid Y spacing** are also equal. If you want this to continue, make sure that the checkbox **Equal X and Y spacing** is always checked.
- By default, if you are working with 2D you will only see **Grid** dots. If you work with 3D, you will see **Grid** lines; therefore, you must set the **Major line** spacing.
- Also, all of the settings of **Grid behavior** are meant for 3D drawings.
- Make sure that **Snap type** is **Grid snap** (we will discuss **Polar Snap** shortly). If you are creating a 2D drawing, then select the **Rectangular snap** option. If you are creating a 3D drawing, select **Isometric snap**.
- If you want **Grid** to follow **Snap**, set the two grid values to zero.
- You can use function keys to turn on both **Snap** and **Grid**:
  - F9 = **Snap** on/off
  - F7 = **Grid** on/off

SNAP AND GRID

Exercise 3

1. Start AutoCAD 2010.
2. Open the file *Exercise_03.dwg*.

3. Using **Snap** and **Grid**, draw the following lines without typing any coordinates on the keyboard. Start from the lower left-hand corner with 2.75,2.25 (do not draw the dimensions):

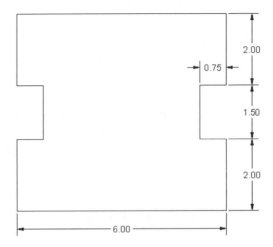

4. Save the file and close it.

■ Change the **Snap X spacing** to 0.25 first and set the grid values to 0. Switch both **Snap** and **Grid** on and draw the lines as required.

2.5 PRECISION METHOD 2: DIRECT DISTANCE ENTRY AND ORTHO

■ Because we know that lines in AutoCAD are **vectors**, we need to specify a length and an angle to successfully draw them.
■ **Ortho** is a tool that will force the cursor to always give us orthogonal angles (i.e., 0, 90, 180, and 270).
■ **Direct Distance Entry** is a very handy tool in drafting; if the mouse is already directed toward an angle, just type in the distance and press [Enter].
■ Combining the two tools will allow us to draw lines with precise lengths and angles.
■ Follow these steps:

- On the **Status Bar**, click the **Ortho Mode** button.

- Start the **Line** command.
- Specify the first point.
- Move the mouse to the right, up, left, and down. Notice how it only gives you orthogonal angles.
- Use the desired angle, type in the distance, and press [Enter].
- Continue with other segments using the same method.

 ▪ You can also use **Direct Distance Entry** with **Dynamic Input**.

DIRECT DISTANCE ENTRY AND ORTHO

 Exercise 4

1. Start AutoCAD 2010.
2. Open file *Exercise_04.dwg*.
3. Using **Ortho** and **Direct Distance Entry**, draw the shape that follows starting from the lower left-hand corner with 3,2 (without dimensions):

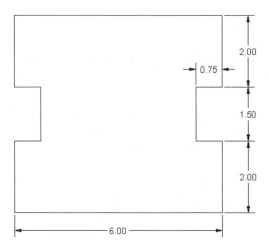

4. Save the file and close it.

2.6 THE ARC COMMAND

- The **Arc** command is used to draw circular arcs (the arc part of a circle).
- Take a look at the following illustration:

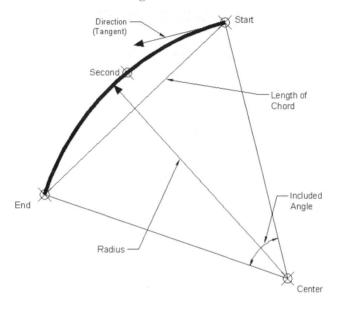

- The information that AutoCAD recognizes about an arc includes:
  - Start point
  - Second point (not necessarily the midpoint)
  - Endpoint
  - Center point
  - Radius
  - Length of chord
  - Included angle (angle between **Start**, **Center**, **End**)
  - Direction (the tangent passes through the start point)
- AutoCAD only needs three pieces of information to draw an arc, but not just any three.
- AutoCAD will start asking you to make your first input, choosing either the start point or the center point, and based on that choice it will ask you to specify the second piece of information, and so on.

- Make sure you are in the **Home** tab on the **Ribbon**, and, using the **Draw** panel, click the **Arc** button (the small arrow at the right). You will see the following:

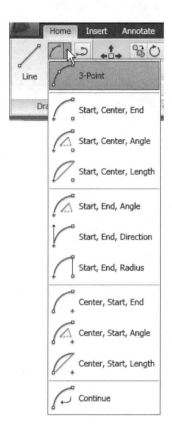

- Before you start, specify the desired method from the menu and AutoCAD will take it from there.

 ■ Always think counterclockwise (CCW) when specifying points.

DRAWING ARCS

 Exercise 5

1. Start AutoCAD 2010.
2. Open the file *Exericise_05.dwg*. You will see the following shape:

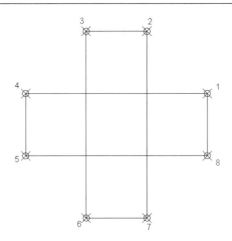

3. Turn on **Snap** and **Grid**.

4. Draw the first arc between point (1) and (2) using **Start**, **End**, **Angle**, where point (1) is the start point and the angle = –90.

5. Draw the second arc between point (3) and (4) using **Start**, **End**, **Direction**, where point (3) is the start point and the direction = 270.

6. Draw the third arc between point (5) and (6) using **Start**, **Center**, **End**, where point (6) is the start point and the point at the lower left is the center point (you can specify it using **Snap** and **Grid**).

7. Draw the fourth arc between point (7) and (8) using **Start**, **Center**, **Length**, where point (8) is the start point, the point at the lower right is the center point, and the length of the chord is the distance between (8) and (7).

8. The shape should look like this:

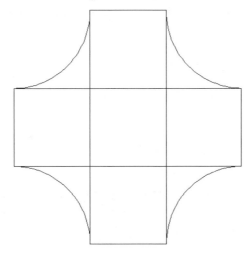

9. Save the file and close it.

2.7 THE CIRCLE COMMAND

- The **Circle** command is used to draw a circle.
- There are six different methods available to draw a circle in AutoCAD.
- To use the first two methods you have to know the center of the circle. They are:

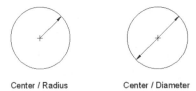

Center / Radius   Center / Diameter

- To use the third method, select three points opposite each other (see the following illustration) on the perimeter of the circle.
- To use the fourth method, specify two points opposite each other on the perimeter of the circle. The distance between them is equal to the diameter.

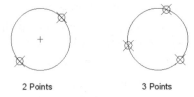

2 Points   3 Points

- To use the fifth method, you should have two objects already drawn—we can consider them as tangents—then specify a radius.
- To use the sixth method, you should specify three tangents by selecting three objects.

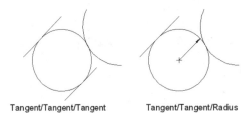

Tangent/Tangent/Tangent   Tangent/Tangent/Radius

- Make sure you are in the **Home** tab on the **Ribbon**, and, using the **Draw** panel, click the **Circle** button (the small arrow at the right). You will see the following:

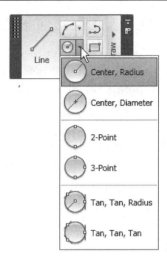

- Before you start, specify the desired method from the menu and AutoCAD will take it from there.

DRAWING A CIRCLE

Exercise 6

1. Start AutoCAD 2010.
2. Open the file *Exericise_06.dwg*.
3. Make sure that **Snap** and **Grid** are on.
4. Draw the five circles, which should look like the following:

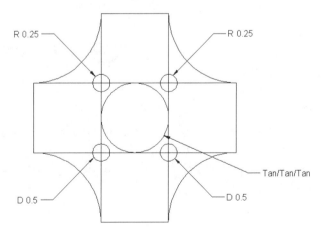

5. Save the file and close it.

2.8 PRECISION METHOD 3: OBJECT SNAP (OSNAP)

- AutoCAD keeps a full record of each object in each drawing.
- **Object Snap (OSNAP)** is a tool that helps you utilize these records when you need to specify points on objects already precisely drawn without knowing the points.
- For example,
  - Assume we have the following shape:

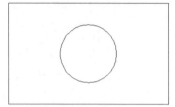

  - We have no information about any object in this shape.
  - We were asked to draw a precise line from the midpoint of the right line to the tangent to the top of the circle.
  - The command to draw is **Line**. AutoCAD asked us to specify the first point and we typed **mid** and pressed [Enter] (or [Spacebar]), then went directly to the upper line and a yellow triangle appeared. We clicked:

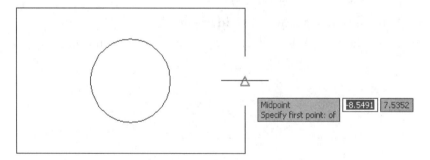

  - AutoCAD then asked us to specify the next point. We typed **tan** and pressed [Enter] (or [Spacebar]), then went directly to the top of the circle and a yellow circle appeared. We clicked it and then pressed [Enter] to end the command:

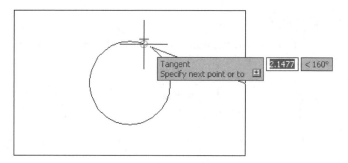

- Mission accomplished.

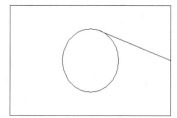

- Some of the **OSNAPs** are used to catch the following:
  - The endpoint of an object
  - The midpoint of an object
  - The intersection of two objects
  - The center of an arc or a circle
  - The quadrant of an arc or a circle
  - The tangent of an arc or a circle
  - The perpendicular point on an object
  - A point on an object nearest to your click point
- We will discuss more **OSNAPs** as we learn additional commands.
- There are three ways to use the **OSNAPs** whenever you are asked to specify a point, these include: Typing, [Shift] + right-click, Running **OSNAP**.

Typing

- Type the first three letters of the desired **OSNAP** such as, **end**, **mid**, **cen**, **qua**, **int**, **per**, **tan**, and **nea**. This is a very old method, but often used among seasoned users of AutoCAD.

[Shift] + Right-click

- Hold the [Shift] key and right-click. The following menu will appear. Select the desired **OSNAP**.

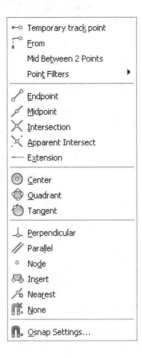

Running OSNAP

- This method is the most practical method of those we have mentioned.
- You will select an **OSNAP** and it will run all the time. The next time you are asked to specify an endpoint, for example, simply go to the desired point and it will be acquired immediately.
- There are two ways to activate running **OSNAP**:
  - On the **Status Bar**, right-click the **OSNAP** button and the following menu will appear:

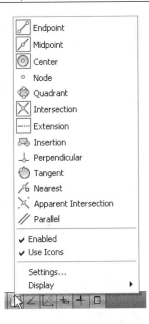

- In this example, **Endpoint**, **Midpoint**, **Center**, **Intersection**, and **Extension**, are all running (each icon has a frame around it).
- You can also select **Settings** and the following dialog box will appear:

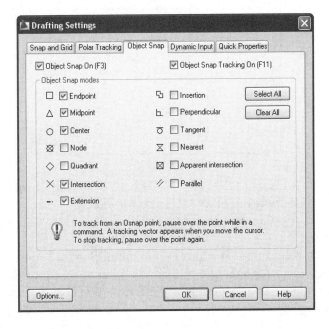

- Switch on the desired **OSNAP** and click **OK**.

2.9 OBJECT SNAP TRACKING (OTRACK)

- If you have a rectangle, and you want to draw a circle where its center will coincide with the exact center of the rectangle, **Object Snap Tracking (OTRACK)** will help you do this without drawing any new objects to facilitate specifying the exact points.
- **OTRACK** uses **OSNAP**s of existing objects to steal the coordinates of the new point.
- On the **Status Bar**, click the **OTRACK** button.

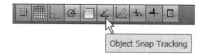

- Make sure that **OSNAP** is also on, as **OTRACK** alone would not do anything.

Example of Two-points **OTRACK**

- Let's look at an example where we will use two points to specify one point.
  - Assume we have the following rectangle:

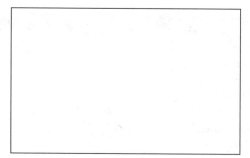

  - Make sure that **OSNAP** and **OTRACK** are both turned on. Make sure that **Midpoint** in **OSNAP** is also turned on.
  - Start the **Circle** command, which will ask you to specify the center point.
  - Go to the upper (or lower) horizontal line and move to the midpoint and hover for a couple of seconds, then move up or down. You will see an infinite line extending in both directions (do not click), just like the following:

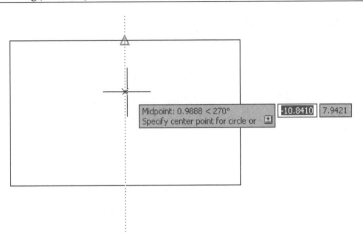

- Go to the right (or left) vertical line and move to the midpoint and hover for couple of seconds, then move right or left. You will see an infinite line extending in both directions, just like the following:

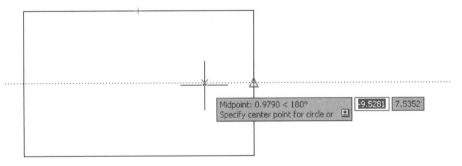

- Now, move your cursor to where you think the two infinite lines should intersect:

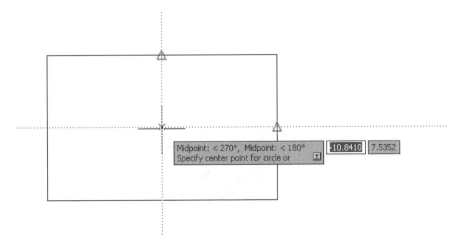

- Once you see the two infinite lines, click. You have specified the center point of the circle. You can now type in the radius (diameter) of the circle:

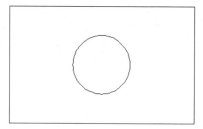

Example of One-point **OTRACK**

- Let's look at another example. This time we will use one point to specify one point:
  - Continue with the same rectangle used in the last example.
  - Start the **Circle** command, which will ask you to specify the center point.
  - Make sure both **OSNAP** and **OTRACK** are turned on, and also turn on **Center** in **OSNAP**.
  - Go to the center point of the existing circle, and hover for couple of seconds, then move to the right. An infinite line will appear:

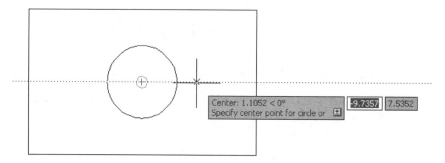

- Type 2 (or any distance) and press [Enter]:

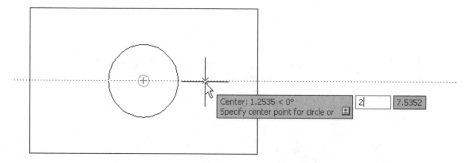

- The center of the new circle will be specified, then type in the radius. You will see the following:

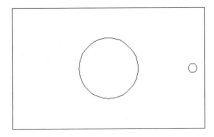

■ If you hover over a point for couple of seconds to produce the infinite line and then discover that it is not the desired point, simply go to the same point again, and hover over it for a couple of seconds to disable it.

DRAWING USING OSNAP AND OTRACK

Exercise 7

1. Start AutoCAD 2010.

2. Open the file *Exercise_07.dwg*.

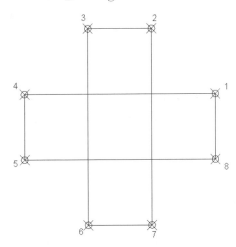

3. Make sure that **Snap** and **Grid** are both turned off.

4. Using **OSNAP**, switch on **Endpoint**.

5. Draw the first arc between points (1) and (2) using **Start**, **End**, **Angle**, where point (1) is the start point and the angle = –90.

6. Draw the second arc between points (3) and (4) using **Start**, **End**, **Direction**, where point (3) is the start point and the direction = 270.

7. Draw the third arc between points (5) and (6) using **Start**, **Center**, **End**, where point (6) is the start point. To specify the center point, use **OTRACK** between points (5) and (6).

8. Draw the fourth arc between points (7) and (8) using **Start**, **Center**, **Length**, where point (8) is the start point. To specify the center point, use **OTRACK** between points (7) and (8), where the length of the chord is the distance between (8) and (7).

9. The shape should look like the following:

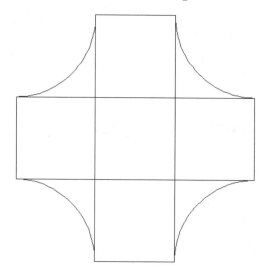

10. Using **OSNAP**, turn **Intersection** on. Use **Intersection** to specify the center points for the five small circles. (By default, AutoCAD will activate **Tangent** when you use the **Tan**, **Tan**, **Tan** method.)

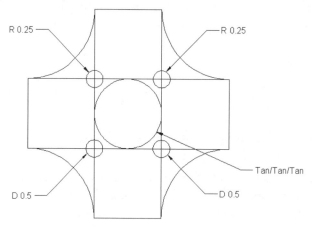

11. Save the file and close it.

DRAWING USING OSNAP AND OTRACK

Exercise 8
1. Start AutoCAD 2010.
2. Open the file *Exercise_08.dwg*.
3. Turn **OSNAP** on and set the following: **Endpoint**, **Midpoint**, and **Center**.
4. Turn on **OTRACK**.
5. Draw the four circles and specify the center using **OSNAP** and **OTRACK**.

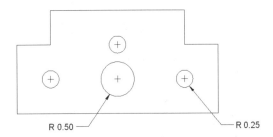

6. Save the file and close it.

2.10 THE PLINE COMMAND

- Pline means "polyline" and poly means many—so, if you exchange many with poly, the new name would be "many lines."
- To begin, let's compare the **Line** command and the **Pline** command.

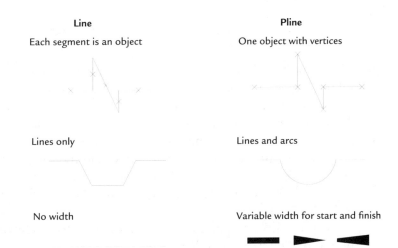

- As you can see from the comparison, there are mainly three differences between the two commands.
- Make sure you are in the **Home** tab on the **Ribbon**, and, using the **Draw** panel, click the **Polyline** button:

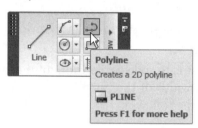

- The following prompt will appear:

```
Specify start point:
Current line-width is 0.9000
Specify next point or [Arc/Halfwidth/Length/Undo/Width]:
```

- After you specify the first point, the **Pline** command will give you the current polyline width (in our example it is 0.90), then it will ask you to specify the next point. You can use all of the methods we learned in the **Line** command.
- If you do not want to specify the second point, you can choose from the following: **Arc**, **Halfwidth**, **Length**, and **Width**.

Arc

- By default, the **Pline** command will draw lines.
- You can change the mode to draw arcs by selecting the **Arc** option. The following prompt will appear:

```
Specify endpoint of arc or
[Angle/Center/Close/Direction/Halfwidth/Line/Radius/Second pt/
Undo/Width]:
```

- We learned in the **Arc** command that AutoCAD needs three pieces of information to draw an arc.
- AutoCAD already knows the start point of the arc, which is the start point of the polyline or the endpoint of the last line segment.
- AutoCAD will assume that the direction of the arc will be the same angle as the last line segment. Users have the right to accept or reject this assumption.
- If you accept this assumption, then AutoCAD will ask you to specify the endpoint of the arc.
- If you reject this assumption, then you will need to specify the second piece of information from the following:

- Angle of arc, then center or radius
- Center, then angle or length
- Direction, then end
- Radius, then end or angle
- Second, then end

Halfwidth

- The first method is to specify the width of the polyline.
- Specify the halfwidth of the polyline from the center to one of its edges, something like the following:

- When you select this option, AutoCAD will give you the following prompt:

```
Specify starting half-width <1.0000>:
Specify ending half-width <1.0000>:
```

- In this example, the halfwidth was 1.0 for both the start point and endpoint.

Length

- In the **Pline** command, if you draw an arc, then switch to the **Line** command to draw a line segment, and if you want the line to be tangent to the arc, then select this option.
- This option will assume the angle to be the same of the last segment, hence, you will only be asked for the length. The following prompt will appear:

```
Specify length of line:
```

Width

- Width is the same as halfwidth, but instead, you have to input the full width. See the following illustration:

- The **Undo** and **Close** options are the same options as in the **Line** command.
- If you choose to close in the **Arc** option, it will close the shape by an arc.

DRAWING POLYLINES

Exercise 9

1. Start AutoCAD 2010.
2. Open the file *Exercise_09.dwg*.
3. Using **Ortho** and **Direct Distance Entry**, draw the following shape (without dimensions) using the **Pline** command with width = 0.1.

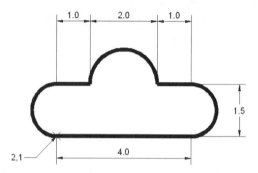

4. Save the file and close it.

■ Take note of the following tips:
   • In order to draw the large arc, use angle = 180.
   • Before you draw the last arc, change the mode to **Arc** and select **Close**.

2.11 POLAR TRACKING

■ We learned that we can force the cursor to give us four orthogonal angles (0, 90, 180, 270) using **ORTHO**.
■ If we want other angles, such as 30 and its multiples or 60 and its multiples, **ORTHO** would not help us. For this reason, AutoCAD provides another powerful tool called **Polar Tracking**.
■ **Polar Tracking** allows you to have rays starting from your current point pointing toward angles such as 30, 60, 90, 120, and so on. You can use **Direct Distance Entry** just as we did with **ORTHO**.
■ On the **Status Bar**, click the **Polar Tracking** button.

- In order to select the desired angle, right click on the button and you will see the following menu:

- Select the desired angle and you will get it, along with its multiples.
- If you want more control, right-click on the button and select **Settings**. The following dialog box will appear:

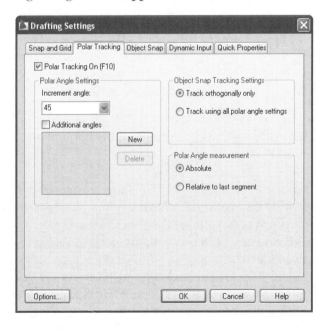

- Under **Polar Angle Settings**, select the **Increment angle** (a list in a drop-down menu where you will find predefined angles). Select the desired angle.

- If the desired angle is not on the list, simply type your own angle.
- Based on this example, users will have rays in angles 0, 30, 60, 90, 120, etc.

Additional Angles

- Sometimes, in the design process, you will need some odd angles that the **Increment angle** option cannot give you, such as 95 or 115.
- The **Additional angles** option will help you set these odd angles.
- Using the same dialog box, check the **Additional angles** box.
- Click the **New** button and type in the angle.
- To delete an existing additional angle, select it and click the **Delete** button.
- You will have something similar to the following:

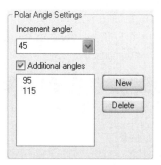

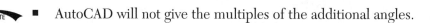 AutoCAD will not give the multiples of the additional angles.

Polar Snap

- We previously discussed the **SNAP** command, which helped us to specify exact points on the X,Y plane using the mouse.
- The **SNAP** command can only help us along the X-axis (+ and −), and along the Y-axis (+ and −).
- If you want to snap to a point along a ray produced by **Polar Snap**, you have to change the type of the **SNAP** from **Grid Snap** to **Polar Snap**.
- On the **Status Bar**, switch on **SNAP**. Right-click on the **SNAP** button and select **Settings**. Under **Snap type**, select **Polar Snap** instead of **Grid Snap**, just like the following:

- Now, set the **Polar spacing** value, just like the following:

Example

- We want to draw the following shape:

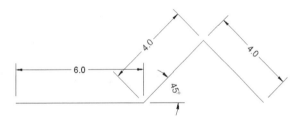

- Let's assume we set the **Increment angle** to 45 and we changed the type of **Snap** to **Polar Snap** with a distance = 1.0. The following steps show you how to draft using **Polar Tracking**:
  - Start the **Line** command, then specify a starting point.
  - Move to the right until you see the ray. Read the distance and the angle. When you reach your distance, click to specify a point just like the following:

- Move the cursor toward the angle 45 until you see the ray. Then, move the mouse to the desired distance and click:

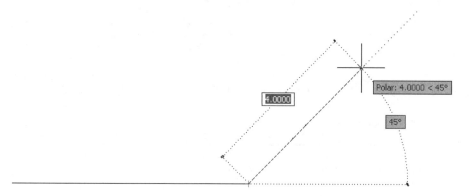

- Move the cursor toward the angle 315 until you see the ray. Then, move the mouse to the desired distance and click:

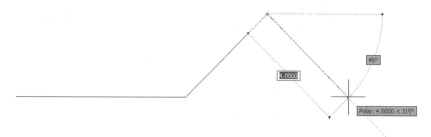

DRAWING USING POLAR TRACKING

Exercise 10

1. Start AutoCAD 2010.
2. Open the file *Exercise_10.dwg*.
3. Switch both **Polar Tracking** and **Polar Snap** on and set the following:
    a. Increment angle = 30
    b. Additional angles = 135
    c. Polar distance = 0.5
4. Draw the following shape (without dimensions) starting from 3,2:

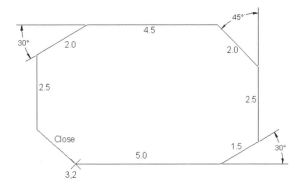

5. Save the file and close it.

2.12 THE ERASE COMMAND

- The **Erase** command will be the first modifying command we discuss.
- The only purpose of this command is to delete any object you select.
- Make sure you are in the **Home** tab on the **Ribbon**, and, using the **Modify** panel, click the **Erase** button.

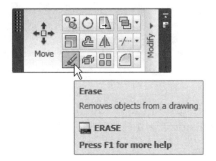

- The following prompt will appear:
```
Select objects:
```

- Once this prompt appears the cursor will change to a pick box:

- Basically, you can do three things with the pick box:
    - Touch an object and click to select it.
    - Go to an empty place, click, and go to the right; this will get you a **Window**.
    - Go to an empty place, click, and go to the left; this will get you a **Crossing**.

Window

- A window is a rectangle specified by two opposite corners (points). The first point will be placed when you click on the empty place. Then, release your hand, go to a suitable place, and click the second point to create the opposite corner.

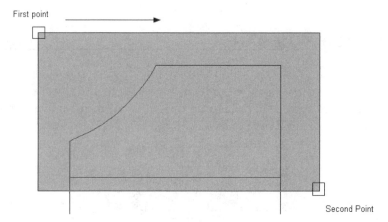

- Whatever is fully inside the rectangle will be selected. If any part (even a small part) is outside the rectangle it will not be selected. See the following illustration:

Crossing

- A crossing is just like a window, except that whatever is inside it will be selected in addition to whatever it touches.

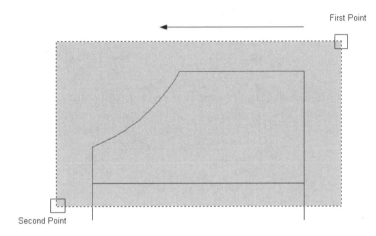

- The result will be:

 ■ These three methods can be used with almost all of the modifying commands, not just the **Erase** command.
- The **Select Objects** prompt is repetitive. You need to always finish by pressing [Enter] or you can right-click and use the menu.
- Other ways to erase objects are:
  - Without issuing any command, click on the desired object(s) and press the [Del] key.

- Without issuing any command, click on the desired object(s), then right-click, and the following shortcut menu will appear. Select **Erase**.

2.13 OOPS, UNDO, AND REDO COMMANDS

- This group of commands can help you correct your mistakes.
- They can be used in the current session only (i.e., once you close the file, they will be useless).

Oops

- **Oops** is used to retain the last group of erased objects.
- **Oops** only works with the **Erase** command.
- This command is only available in the **Command Window**.
- You have to type the full command in the **Command Window**: **Oops**.
- No prompt will be displayed, but you will see the last group of erased objects returned to the drawing.

Undo

- **Undo** is used to undo the last command.
- You can reach this command using one of the following methods:
  - From the **Quick Access** toolbar, click the **Undo** button:

  - Type **u** in the **Command Window** (don't type **undo**, because it has a different meaning).
  - Press [Ctrl] + Z.
- The last command will be undone.
- You can undo as many commands as you want in the current session.

Redo

- This command is used to undo the undo.
- You can use this command using one of the following methods:
  - From the **Quick Access** toolbar, click the **Redo** button.

  - Type **redo** in the **Command Window**.
  - Or press [Ctrl] + Y.
- The last undone command will be redone.
- You can redo as many commands as you want in the current session.

2.14 REDRAW AND REGEN COMMANDS

- There are times when you need to refresh the screen for one reason or another.
- Sometimes you will need AutoCAD to regenerate the whole drawing to show the arcs and circles as smooth curves.
- Neither command has a toolbar button.

Redraw

- From the **Menu Browser**, select **View/Redraw** or type **r** in the **Command Window**.
- The screen will be refreshed.

Regen

- From the **Menu Browser**, select **View/Regen** or type **re** in the **Command Window**.
- See the following example:
  - This is how the drawing looks before the **Regen** command:

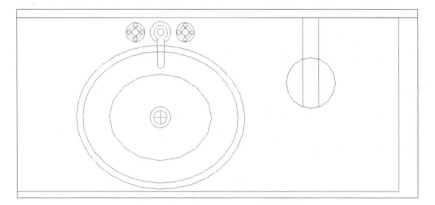

  - This is how the drawing looks after the **Regen** command:

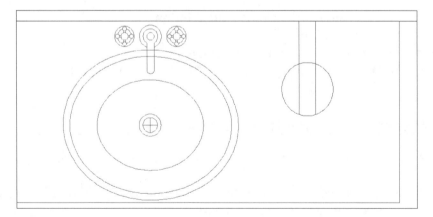

  - Notice the lines are smoother.

ERASE, OOPS, UNDO, AND REDO

Exercise 11

1. Start AutoCAD 2010.
2. Open the file *Exercise_11.dwg*.
3. Using the **Erase** command with **Window** or **Crossing**, perform the following steps:
   a. Using **Window**, try to erase all of the rectangles in the middle. Press [Enter], then use the **Oops** command to retain the objects.
   b. Using **Crossing**, try to erase the circles on the right-hand side of the shape. Press [Enter] and then **Undo**. Also, try **Redo** to see the effect.
   c. Using a pick box, try to erase the lines of the frame. Press [Enter] and then use **Undo** to undo the erasing.
4. Close the file without saving.

CHAPTER REVIEW

1. Which of the following statements are true:
   a. **Snap** will help us control the mouse whereas **Grid** is complementary to **Snap**.
   b. **Ortho** and **Direct Distance Entry** will help us draw exact orthogonal lines.
   c. You can use **Direct Distance Entry** with **Dynamic Input**, **Ortho**, and **Polar Tracking**.
   d. All of the above.
2. The **Arc** command in AutoCAD will draw a _____ arc.
3. Using **OTRACK**, you can:
   a. Specify a point using two existing points.
   b. Specify the radius of an arc.
   c. Specify the end of an existing line.
   d. None of the above.
4. **OTRACK** doesn't need **OSNAP** to work.
   a. True
   b. False

5. In **Polar Tracking**, if the **Increment angle** option did not fulfill all your
    needs:
    a. **Ortho** will help.
    b. Set the additional angles.
    c. The command **PolarNewAngles** will help.
    d. None of the above.
6. There are _____ ways to draw a circle in AutoCAD.

CHAPTER REVIEW ANSWERS

1. d
2. circular
3. a
4. b
5. b
6. six

Chapter 3

HOW TO SET UP YOUR DRAWING

In This Chapter
◊ Things to Consider before You Set Up Your Drawing
◊ Step 1: Drawing Units
◊ Step 2: Drawing Limits
◊ Step 3: Creating Layers
◊ Layer Functions
◊ **Quick Properties, Properties,** and **Match Properties**

3.1 THINGS TO CONSIDER BEFORE YOU SET UP YOUR DRAWING

- There are many things you will need to think about when you set up your drawing file. Of course, we cannot cover them all in this chapter, but we will cover the most important things.

Drawing Units

- We will first define the drawing distance and angle units, along with their precision.

Drawing Limits

- Try to figure out what size (area) workspace will be sufficient to accommodate your drawing.

Layers

- Layers are the most effective way to organize your drawings, so we will learn what they are, how to create them, and how to control them.

■ In Appendix A, we will discuss ways to create templates in AutoCAD®, which are more applicable for businesses than individuals.

3.2 STEP 1: DRAWING UNITS

- ■ First, you will learn how to draw units.
- ■ This command will allow you to select the proper length and angle units.
- ■ From the **Application Menu** select **Drawing/Units**:

■ After you make your selection, the following dialog box will appear:

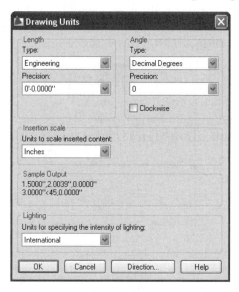

■ Under **Length**, set the desired **Type**. You will have five choices:
  • Architectural (example: 1'-5 3/16")
  • Decimal (example: 20.4708)
  • Engineering (example: 1'-4.9877")
  • Fractional (example: 17 1/16)
  • Scientific (example: 1.6531E+01)
■ Under **Angle**, set the desired **Type**. You will have five choices:
  • Decimal Degrees (example: 45.5)
  • Deg/Min/Sec (example: 45d30'30")
  • Grads (example: 50.6g)
  • Radians (example: 0.8r)
  • Surveyor's Units (example: N 45d30'30" E)
■ For the desired **Length** and **Angle**, select the **Precision**, for example:
  • Architectural precision can be 0'−0 1/16", 0'−0 1/32", etc.
  • Decimal precision can be 0.00, 0.000, etc.
  • Deg/Min/Sec precision can be 0d00'00", 0d00'00.0", etc.
■ By default, AutoCAD deals with the positive angles counterclockwise. If you prefer it the other way around, check the **clockwise** box.

- Under **Insertion scale**, specify **Units to scale inserted content**, which is your drawing's scale against the scale of any object (a block, for example). This will help AutoCAD make the suitable conversion.
- Click the **Direction** button to see the following dialog box:

- As we discussed in Chapter 1, AutoCAD always starts the zero angle measuring from the east. If you want to change the direction, select the desired angle to be considered as the new zero.

3.3 STEP 2: DRAWING LIMITS

- In Chapter 1, we learned that AutoCAD offers an unlimited drawing sheet, which extends in all directions. We will not use it all, instead we will specify an area that gives us our **limits**.
- **Drawing Limits** is the workspace you select to work in and can be specified using two points: the lower left-hand corner and the upper right-hand corner.
- Since we will draw in **Model Space** and print from **Paper Space**, we do not need to think about drawing scale at this point.
- To know the exact limits needed, make sure you have the following information:
  - What is the longest dimension in your sketch in both the X-axis and Y-axis?
  - What AutoCAD unit have you selected (e.g., meter, centimeter, millimeter, inch, foot, etc.)?
- Accordingly, you will know the limit of your drawing.

Example

- Assume we have the following case:
  - We want to draw an architectural plan, which extends in X for 50 m and in Y for 30 m.
  - Also, assume that one AutoCAD unit = 1 m.

- If one AutoCAD unit = 1 m, then 50 m is equal to 50 AutoCAD units, which also applies to 30 m.
- Note that 0,0 is always the common lower left-hand corner, so there is no need to change it. The upper right-hand corner will be 50,30.
- At the command prompt, type **limits**, the following prompt will appear in the **Command Window**:

```
Specify lower left corner or [ON/OFF] <0,0>: (press [Enter]
to accept the default value) Specify upper right corner
<12,9>: (type in the coordinate of the upper right corner)
```

- To keep yourself from using any area outside this limit, turn on the **Limits**.

DRAWING UNITS AND LIMITS

 Exercise 12

1. Start AutoCAD 2010.
2. Open the file *Exercise_12.dwg*.
3. Note the current units (look at the lower left-hand corner of the screen and you will see the coordinates of the drawing).
4. From the **Application Menu** select **Drawing/Units**. Change the units to be:
   a. Length Type = Architectural
   b. Length Precision = 0'-0 1/32"
   c. Angle Type = Deg/Min/Sec
   d. Angle Precision = 0d00'00"
5. Now, check the coordinates again and see how the numbers have changed with the new units.
6. Using the **Limits** command, do the following:
   a. Accept the default point for the lower left-hand corner.
   b. For the upper right-hand corner type **30',20'**.
7. Switch **Grid** on and double-click on the mouse wheel.
8. You will see your current settings.
9. Save and close the file.

3.4 STEP 3: CREATING LAYERS

What Are Layers?

- Let's assume that we have a large number of transparent papers along with 256 colored pens.
- Taking care that we do not draw anywhere except on the top of the paper, we select the red pen and draw the border of the drawing.
- Then, we move the second paper to the top, and we draw an architectural wall plan using the yellow pen.
- Next, we move the third paper to the top and we draw the doors using the green pen. Employing the same procedure we draw windows, furniture, electrical outlets, hatching, text, dimensioning, etc.
- Then, we take all of the papers and look at them at the same time. What do we see? A full architectural plan!
- In AutoCAD we call each paper a layer.
- Each layer should have a name, color, linetype, lineweight, and much more information.
- There will be a layer, which will be in all of AutoCAD's drawings. This layer is 0 (zero). You cannot delete it or rename it.
- In order to draw on a layer, you must first make it **current**. Only one layer will be current at a time.
- The objects drawn on a layer will automatically inherit the properties (color, linetype, lineweight, etc.) of the current layer. Hence, a line in the red layer, with a dashdot linetype and 0.3 lineweight will have the exact same properties.
- By default, the setting of the object's color is = BYLAYER.
- By default, the setting of the object's linetype is = BYLAYER.
- By default, the setting of the object's lineweight is = BYLAYER.
- NOTE ▸ It is highly recommended to keep these settings intact, as changing them may lead to creating objects with nonstandard properties.
- On the **Ribbon**, make sure you are in the **Home** tab. Using the **Layers** panel, click the **Layer Properties** button.

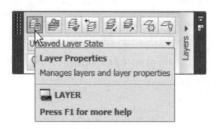

- The following dialog box will appear:

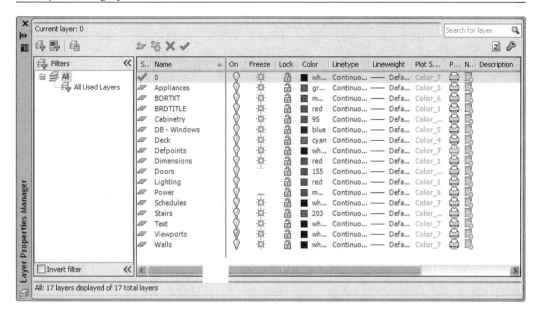

- The **Layer Properties** is not a normal dialog box; rather, it is a palette that can be docked, resized, and hidden.
  - Drag the title of the palette to the right, left, top, or bottom of the screen and you will see the **Layer Properties** palette change its size and dock at the place you select.
  - You can hide the entire palette and show only the title bar by clicking the **Auto-hide** button as shown in the following. Whenever you want to see the palette again, simply go back to the title and the palette will appear.

  - You can show the **Properties** menu to control the palette. Click the **Properties** button as shown.

- The following menu will appear:

- The most important options available in this menu are **Anchor Left** and **Anchor Right**, which automatically dock the palette at the right or at the left and will switch on **Auto-hide**.
- You can resize the palette to be larger or smaller. Move to the lower right-hand corner of the palette; the cursor will change to the following:

- Click and drag to the right to make it larger. Click and drag it to the left to make it smaller.

Creating a New Layer

- To create a new layer in the drawing, you must prepare all of the necessary information for the new layer.
- Click the **New Layer** button.

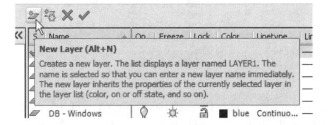

- AutoCAD will add a new layer with the temporary name *Layer1*. The **Name** field will be highlighted. Type the desired name of the layer (you can use up to 255 characters and spaces are allowed). Only use the following:

- Letters (a, b, c, …, z); lowercase or uppercase doesn't matter
- Numbers (0, 1, 2, …, 9)
- Hyphen (-), underscore (_), and dollar sign ($)

■ It is a common practice to use good layer naming, using a name that gives an idea about the contents of the layer. For example, a layer that contains the walls of a building would be named "wall."

Setting a Color for a Layer

■ After you create a layer, set its color.
■ AutoCAD uses 256 colors for the layers (as a matter of fact, there are only 255 if we exclude the color of the **Graphical Area**).
■ The first seven colors can be called by their names or numbers:
- Red (1)
- Yellow (2)
- Green (3)
- Cyan (4)
- Blue (5)
- Magenta (6)
- Black/White (7)
■ The remaining colors can only be called by their numbers.
■ You can have the same color for more than one layer.
■ Select the desired layer under the **Color** field, and click either the name of the color or the icon. The following dialog box will appear:

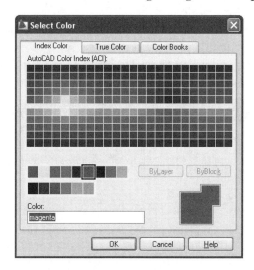

■ Move to the desired color (or type in the name/number) and then click **OK**.

■ You can also set the layer's color through the pop-up list in the **Layers** panel by selecting the color icon in the list:

Setting a Linetype for a Layer

■ AutoCAD comes with a good number of generic predefined linetypes saved in a couple of files called *acad.lin* and *acadiso.lin*.

■ You can also buy other linetypes from third parties, which can be found on the Internet. Just go to any search engine and search for "AutoCAD linetype." You will find many linetype files, some free of charge and some you can buy for few dollars.

■ Not all linetypes are loaded in the drawing files; you may need to load the desired linetype first before you can use it.

■ First, select the desired layer. Under the field **Linetype**, click the name of the linetype and the following dialog box will appear:

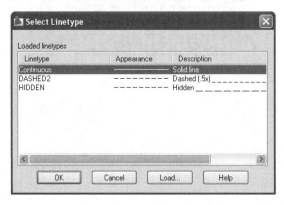

- If your desired linetype is there, select it. To load another linetype, click the **Load** button and the following dialog box will appear:

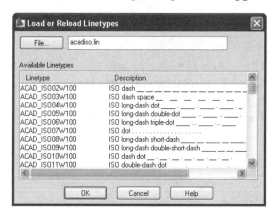

- Select the desired linetype to be loaded and click **OK**. Now that the linetype is loaded, it will appear in the **Select Linetype** dialog box. Select it and click **OK**.

Setting a Lineweight for a Layer

- Select the desired layer under the field **Lineweight**. Click either the number or the shape of the lineweight and the following dialog box will appear:

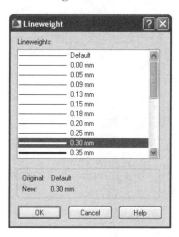

- Select the desired lineweight and click **OK**.
- If you want to view the lineweight of any layer on the screen, click the **Show/ Hide Lineweight** on the **Status Bar**.

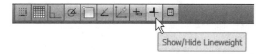

■ We prefer to see the lineweight using **Plot Style** (to be discussed later), which will affect the hardcopy.

Making a Layer the Current Layer

■ There are three ways to make a particular layer the current layer:
- In the **Layer Properties Manager** dialog box, double-click on the name or the status of the desired layer.
- In the **Layer Properties Manager** dialog box, select the desired layer and click the **Set Current** button.

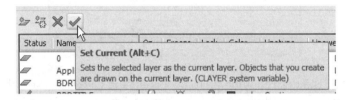

- On the **Ribbon**, make sure you are in the **Home** tab, and, using the **Layers** panel, you will find a pop-up list for the layers. Select the desired layer name and it will become the current layer:

LAYER NAMES, COLORS, LINETYPES, AND LINEWEIGHTS

Exercise 13

1. Start AutoCAD 2010.
2. Open the file *Exercise_13.dwg*.
3. Create the following layers:

Layer Name	Color	Linetype	Lineweight
Shaft	Magenta	Continuous	0.3
Body	Cyan	Continuous	0.3
Base	Green	Continuous	0.3
Centerlines	9	Dashdot2	0.5

4. Make Centerlines the current layer. (Make sure **Dynamic Input** is turned off.)
5. Draw a line from 6,7.5 to 6,4.5. Draw another line from 8,6 to 4,6.
6. Save the file and close it.

3.5 LAYER FUNCTIONS

Adding More Layers

- The easiest way to add more layers is to click on the name of any layer while you are in the **Layer Properties Manager** dialog box and then press [Enter].
- Accordingly, you can use the **New Layer** button.

- By default, AutoCAD will always sort the layers according to their names.

Selecting Layers

- All of the following methods will be done in the **Layer Properties Manager** dialog box.

- There are several ways to select layers:
  - To select a single layer, simply click on it.
  - To select multiple nonconsecutive layers, select the first layer, then hold the [Ctrl] key and click on the other layers.
  - To select multiple consecutive layers, select the first layer, then hold the [Shift] button and click on the last layer you wish to select.
  - To select multiple layers all at once, click on an empty area and hold the mouse. Move to the right or left and a rectangle will appear. Cover the layer that you wish to select and release the mouse.
  - To select all layers, press [Ctrl] + A.
  - To unselect a selected layer, hold the [Ctrl] key and click it.

NOTE
- One of the most important advantages in selecting multiple layers is the ability to then set the color, linetype, or lineweight for group of layers in one step.

Deleting a Layer

- You cannot delete a layer that contains objects, so the first step is to empty the layer from any objects in it.
- Using the **Layer Properties Manager** dialog box, select the desired layer (or layers) to be deleted and do one of the following:
  - Press the [Del] key on the keyboard.
  - Click on the **Delete Layer** button.

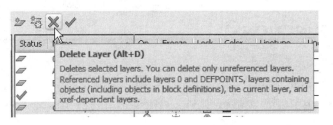

What Happens When You Right-Click?

- Right-clicking here is done in the **Layer Properties Manager** dialog box.

- If you select any layer and right-click, the following shortcut menu will appear:

- Through this shortcut menu you can do many of the things we discussed earlier, such as:
  - Set the current layer
  - Create a new layer
  - Delete a layer
  - Select all layers
  - Clear the selection
  - Select "All but Current"
  - Invert the selection (make the selected unselected, and vice versa)
- The first two choices in this shortcut menu are:
  - **Show Filter Tree** (turned on by default)
  - **Show Filters in Layer List** (turned off by default)

- By turning off the **Show Filter Tree**, the dialog box will have more space, just like the following:

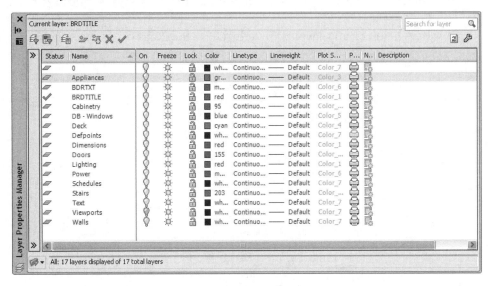

- Or you can you use the two arrows at the left panel, as in the following:

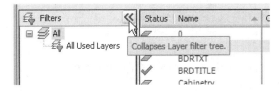

Changing an Object's Layer

- Each object should exist in a layer.
- The fastest way to change the object's layer is the following:
  - Without issuing any command, select the object by clicking it.
  - In the **Layers** toolbar, the object's layer will be displayed. To change it, click the layer's pop-up list and select the new layer.
  - Press the [Esc] key one time.
- Other methods to change an object's layer will be discussed later.

Making an Object's Layer Current

- This function is very useful when there are too many layers in your drawing or you see an object in your drawing, but you do not know in which layer this object resides in.

- What you want to do is to make this object's layer the current layer. To do so you must:
    - Make sure you are in the **Home** tab on the **Ribbon**, and, using the **Layers** panel, click the **Make Object's Layer Current** button.

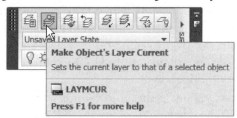

    - The following prompt will appear:

```
Select object whose layer will become current:
(click on the desired object)
Walls is now the current layer.
```

    - Now the current layer is the object's layer.

What Are the Four Switches of a Layer?

- Each layer has four switches, which determine its state.
- You can see these switches in both the **Layer Properties Manager** dialog box and the layer pop-up list from the **Layer** panel.
- These switches are:
    - On/Off
    - Thaw/Freeze
    - Unlock/Lock
    - Plot/No Plot
- See the following example:

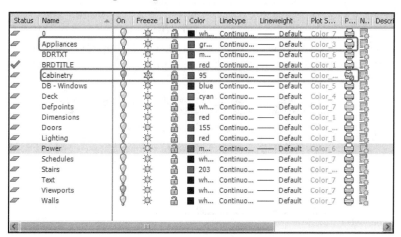

- In the preceding example, you can see that:
  - The **Appliances** layer is On, Thaw, Unlocked, and Plot.
  - The **Cabinetry** layer is Off, Frozen, Locked, and No Plot.
- These four switches are independent from each other.
- By default, the layers are On, Thaw, Unlock, and Plot.
- When you turn a layer off, the objects in it will not be shown on the screen, and if you plot the drawing, the objects will not be plotted. However, the objects in this layer will be counted in the total count of the drawing and the drawing size will not change.
- When you freeze a layer, the objects in it will not be shown on the screen, and if you plot the drawing, the objects will not be plotted. Also, the objects in this layer will not be counted in the total count of the drawing; therefore, the drawing size will be less.
- When you lock a layer, none of the objects in it are modifiable.
- When you make a layer No Plot, you can see the objects on the screen, but when you issue a **Plot** command, these objects will not be plotted.
- Three of these switches can be changed using both the **Layer Properties Manager** dialog box, and the layer pop-up list from the **Layer** panel. The fourth switch, Plot/No Plot, can be changed only from the **Layer Properties Manager** dialog box.
- To change the switch, simply click it.
- NOTE You cannot freeze the current layer, but you can turn it off. See the following dialog box:

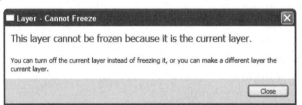

- You should be careful when you turn the current layer off because each and every time you draw a new object it will disappear. Therefore, when you try to turn the current layer off, AutoCAD will issue the following warning message:

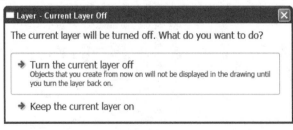

What Is **Layer Previous?**

- While you are working in AutoCAD, you will change the state of layers a lot, which means you need a tool to help you return to the previous state quickly.
- **Layer Previous** helps you do that.
- Make sure you are in the **Home** tab on the **Ribbon**, and, using the **Layers** panel, click the **Previous** button:

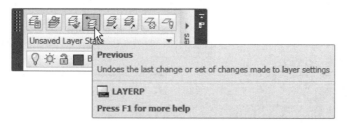

- AutoCAD will report the following statement:

```
Restored previous layer status
```

 - While you are in the **Layer Properties Manager** palette or layer pop-up list from the **Layer** toolbar, and you make several changes on several switches for several layers, AutoCAD considers them all as one action. Thus, they will all be restored in one **Previous** command.

What Is **Layer Match?**

- **Layer Match** converts objects from one layer to another.
- You can use the **Layer Match** tool to help you unify objects belonging to different layers.
- Make sure you are in the **Home** tab on the **Ribbon**, and, using the **Layers** panel, click the **Match** button.

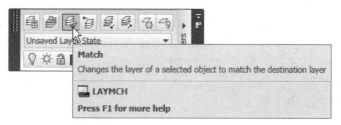

- The following prompt will appear:

```
Select objects to be changed: (Select the desired objects
and once you are done, press [Enter])
Select object on destination layer or [Name]:
```

- Once the command is done, you will see a message similar to this:

```
8 objects changed to layer "Dimensions"
```

LAYER FUNCTIONS

Exercise 14

1. Start AutoCAD 2010.
2. Open the file *Exercise_14.dwg*.
3. Change the object's layers as follows:
    a. Change the layer of the two circles from 0 to Shaft.
    b. Change the layer of the two arcs from 0 to Body.
    c. Change the layer of the lines from 0 to Base.
4. Using the **Status Bar**, switch on **Show/Hide Lineweight**, to see the objects displaying the assigned lineweight.
5. Lock the layer Shaft and then try to erase the objects in it. What message do you receive from AutoCAD?
6. Unlock the layer Shaft.
7. Using the **Make Layer Object's Current** button, select one of the centerlines. Which layer becomes current?
8. Click the **Layer Previous** button twice. What happens?
9. Try to freeze the current layer. What message do you receive from AutoCAD?
10. Try to rename layer 0? What message do you receive from AutoCAD?
11. Rename layer Centerlines to be Center_lines.
12. Try to delete the layer Shaft. What message do you receive from AutoCAD? Why?
13. Save the file and close it.

3.6 QUICK PROPERTIES, PROPERTIES, AND MATCH PROPERTIES

- Earlier in this chapter, we learned that each object inherits the properties of the layer that it resides in. By default, the settings of the current color, linetype, and lineweight is BYLAYER, which means that the object follows the layer it resides in.
- This makes controlling the drawing easier, because it is easier to control a handful of layers than it is to control hundreds of thousands of objects. We recommend you do not change these settings under normal circumstances.
- However, sometimes we may need to change some of the properties. To do that we can use three commands. They are:
  - **Quick Properties**
  - **Properties**
  - **Match Properties**

Quick Properties

- **Quick Properties** is a function that will pop up automatically when you select any object.
- By default, this command is always on, if not, you can turn it on from the **Status Bar**:

- To start the **Quick Properties** command simply click any object and the following small panel will appear:

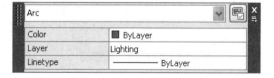

- In this panel you can change the color, layer, and linetype. If you move the mouse over any of the two sides, it will expand just like the following:

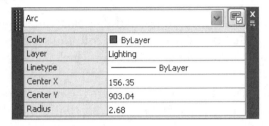

Properties

- The easiest way to initiate the **Properties** command is to select the desired object(s) and then right-click. When the shortcut menu appears, select **Properties**. Now you will be presented with two possibilities:
  - The selection set you made consists of different object types (lines, arcs, circles, etc.). In this case, you can only change the general properties of these objects. The following will appear:

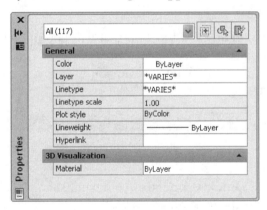

  - However, if you choose the upper pop-up list, you will see the following:

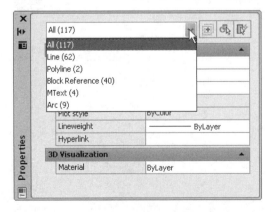

- You can filter the objects you select by selecting the type of object desired. You can change any or all of the properties.
- The selection set you made consists of a single object type. In this case, you can change the general properties and the object-specific properties. The following will appear:

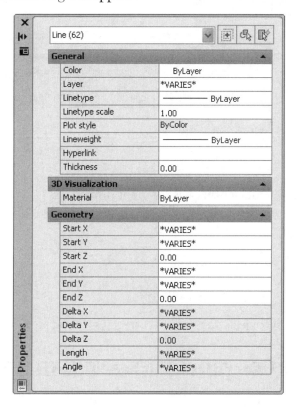

 ■ **Properties** is a palette, which means all the things we learned about the **Layer** palette are applicable here.

Match Properties

- **Match Properties** is useful if you opened a drawing and found that the creator of the drawing did not use the BYLAYER.
- For example, you find a green line residing in a red layer and a dashdot circle in a layer with continuous linetype.
- The best way to correct this is to try to find one object in each layer that has the right properties and then match the other objects to it.

- Make sure you are in the **Home** tab on the **Ribbon**, and, using the **Clipboard** panel, click the **Match Properties** button.

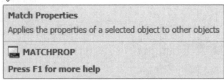

- AutoCAD will give the following prompt:

```
Select source object:
```

- Click on the object that has the right properties.
- The cursor will change to a brush shape:

- AutoCAD will then prompt:

```
Select destination object(s):
```

- Click on the objects you want to correct. Once you are done, press [Enter].

QUICK PROPERTIES, PROPERTIES, AND MATCH PROPERTIES

Exercise 15
1. Start AutoCAD 2010.
2. Open the file *Exercise_15.dwg*.
3. We accidentally drew all objects in layer 0. Using all of the commands you have learned, put each object in its correct layer.
4. Save the file and close it.

CREATING OUR PROJECT (METRIC)

Workshop 1-A
1. Start AutoCAD 2010.
2. Close any open files.
3. Create a new file based on the *acad.dwt* template.

4. Double-click on the mouse wheel to **Zoom Extents**.
5. From the **Application Menu**, select **Drawing/Units** and make the following changes:
    a. Length Type = Decimal, Precision = 0
    b. Angle Type = Decimal Degrees, Precision = 0
    c. Unit to scale inserted content = Millimeters
6. Assume that one AutoCAD unit = 1 mm and you have a 30 x 20 m plan you want to draw. With these measurements, your limits will be:
    a. Lower left-hand corner = 0,0
    b. Upper right-hand corner = 30000,200000
7. Type **Limits** in the **Command Window**, and set the limits accordingly.
8. Double-click on the mouse wheel to **Zoom Extents** to the new limits.
9. Create the following layers:

Layer Name	Color	Linetype	Special Remarks
Frame	Magenta	Continuous	
Walls	Red	Continuous	
Doors	Yellow	Continuous	
Door_Swing	Yellow	Dashed	
Windows	150	Continuous	
Centerlines	Green	Dashdot	
Bubbles	Green	Continuous	
Furniture	41	Continuous	
Staircase	140	Continuous	
Text	Cyan	Continuous	
Hatch	White	Continuous	
Dimension	Blue	Continuous	
Viewports	8	Continuous	No Plot

10. Save the file in the Metric folder (in the copied folder from the DVD) as *Workshop_01.dwg*.

CREATING OUR PROJECT (IMPERIAL)

Workshop 1-B

1. Start AutoCAD 2010.
2. Close any open files.
3. Create a new file based on the *acad.dwt* template.
4. Double-click on the mouse wheel to **Zoom Extents**.
5. From the **Application Menu**, select **Drawing/Units** and make the following changes:
   a. Length Type = Architectural, Precision = 0'-0"
   b. Angle Type = Decimal Degrees, Precision = 0
   c. Unit to scale inserted content = Inches
6. Assume that one AutoCAD unit = 1 inch and you have a 70' x 60' plan you want to draw. With these measurements your limits will be:
   a. Lower left-hand corner = 0,0
   b. Upper right-hand corner = 70',60'
7. Type **Limits** in the **Command Window** and set the limits accordingly.
8. Double-click on the mouse wheel to **Zoom Extents** to the new limits.
9. Create the following layers:

Layer Name	Color	Linetype	Special Remarks
Frame	Magenta	Continuous	
Walls	Red	Continuous	
Doors	Yellow	Continuous	
Door_Swing	Yellow	Dashed	
Windows	150	Continuous	
Centerlines	Green	Dashdot	
Bubbles	Green	Continuous	
Furniture	41	Continuous	
Staircase	140	Continuous	
Text	Cyan	Continuous	
Hatch	White	Continuous	
Dimension	Blue	Continuous	
Viewports	8	Continuous	No Plot

10. Save the file in the Imperial folder (in the copied folder from the DVD) as *Workshop_01.dwg*.

CHAPTER REVIEW

1. Layer names can:
   a. Have up to 255 characters.
   b. Include spaces.
   c. Have letters, numbers, hyphens, underscores, and dollar signs.
   d. All of the above.
2. There are _____ different length units in AutoCAD.
3. What do you need to know to set up limits in a file?
   a. The paper size you will print on.
   b. The longest dimension of your sketch in both X and Y.
   c. The measure of each AutoCAD unit.
   d. B and C.
4. Only the first seven colors can be called by name and number.
   a. True
   b. False
5. What is true about linetypes in AutoCAD?
   a. They are stored in *acad.lin* and *acadiso.lin*.
   b. They are loaded in all AutoCAD drawings.
   c. If I need to use a linetype I have to load it first.
   d. A and C.
6. If you assign a lineweight to a layer, and on this layer you draw lines, you need to click on _____ from the **Status Bar** to see this lineweight on the monitor.
7. You can only change the _____ properties of nonsimilar objects using the **Properties** command.

CHAPTER REVIEW ANSWERS

1. d
2. five
3. d
4. a
5. d
6. **Show/Hide Lineweight** button
7. general

Chapter **4**

A Few Good Construction Commands

In This Chapter

4.1 INTRODUCTION

- So far, we have learned four drawing commands (**Line**, **Arc**, **Circle**, and **Pline**).
- These alone can only help you accomplish 20% of your drawing.
- Also, if you think that each and every line (or arc, or circle) should be drawn by you, you are wrong!
- In this chapter, we will discuss seven commands that will help us construct the most difficult drawings in no time.
- These commands are:
  - The **Offset** command creates parallel copies of your original objects.
  - The **Fillet** command allows you to close unclosed shapes either by extending the two ends to an intersecting point or by using an arc.
  - The **Chamfer** command is exactly the same as the **Fillet** command, except this command will create a slanted edge.
  - The **Trim** command allows some objects to act as cutting edges for other objects to be trimmed.
  - The **Extend** command allows you to extend objects to a boundary.

- The **Lengthen** command allows you to extend or trim length from an existing line.
- The **Join** command allows you to join similar objects (lines to lines, polylines to polylines, etc.).

4.2 THE OFFSET COMMAND

- The **Offset** command will create a new object parallel to a selected object.
- The new object (by default) will have the same properties as the original object and will reside in the same layer.
- There are two methods used in offset:
  - Offset distance
  - Through point
- Make sure you are in the **Home** tab on the **Ribbon**, and, using the **Modify** panel, click the **Offset** button.

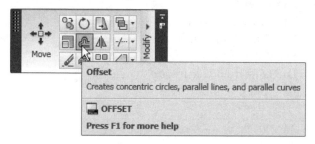

- The following prompt will appear:

```
Current settings: Erase source=No Layer=Source
OFFSETGAPTYPE=0
Specify offset distance or [Through/Erase/Layer]
<Through>:
```

Offset Distance

- If you want to use this method, you should know the distance between the original object and the parallel duplicate (i.e., the offset distance).
- Then, select the object that will be offset.
- Finally, specify the side of the offset by clicking to the right or left, up or down, etc.
- The prompts will be as follows:

```
Specify offset distance or [Through/Erase/Layer]
<Through>: (type in the desired distance)
```

```
Select object to offset or [Exit/Undo] <Exit>:
```
(select a single object)

```
Specify point on side to offset or
[Exit/Multiple/Undo] <Exit>:
```
(click in the desired side)

- The command will repeat the last two prompts for further offsetting.
- To end the command, press [Enter] or right-click.

Through Point

- With this method, there is no need to know the distance but you should know any point that the new parallel object will pass through.
- The prompt will be as follows:

```
Specify offset distance or [Through/Erase/Layer]
<Through>:
```
(type t and press [Enter])
```
Select object to offset or [Exit/Undo] <Exit>:
```
(Select a single object)
```
Specify through point or [Exit/Multiple/Undo] <Exit>:
```
(Specify the point that the new image will pass through)

- The command will repeat the last two prompts for further offsetting.
- To end the command, press [Enter] or right-click.
- Here is an example:

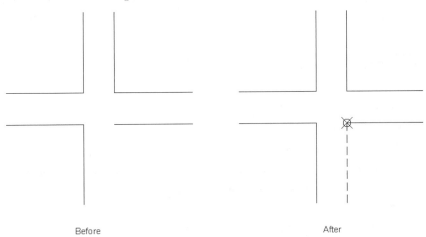

Before   After

Multiple

- With both of the preceding methods you can use the **Multiple** option.
- Instead of repeatedly selecting the object and specifying the side, the **Multiple** option will allow you to specify only the side of the offset.

- The prompt will be as follows:

```
Specify offset distance or [Through/Erase/Layer]
<Through>: (Select either method)
Select object to offset or [Exit/Undo] <Exit>:
(Select a single object)
Specify through point or [Exit/Multiple/Undo] <Exit>:
(Type m and press [Enter])
Specify point on side to offset or [Exit/Undo] <next
object>: (simply click on the desired side, and you can keep
doing the same, once you are done, press [Enter])
```

Undo

- You can use the **Undo** option while you are offsetting to undo the last offsetting action.

 AutoCAD® will recall the last offset distance, so there is no need to keep typing it unless you want to use another value.
- The **Offset** command will produce a bigger or smaller arc, circle, or polyline.
- You can right-click to show shortcut menus displaying the different options of the **Command Window**.
- In the **Offset** command, you can use only one offset distance. If you want another offset distance you must end the current command and issue a new **Offset** command. (We hope to see in the next versions of AutoCAD, **Offset** commands that will allow the user to use more than one offset distance per command.)

OFFSETTING OBJECTS

 Exercise 16
1. Start AutoCAD 2010.
2. Open the file *Exercise_16.dwg*.
3. Offset the walls (magenta) to the inside using the distance = 1'.
4. Offset the stairs using distance = 1'-6" and using the **Multiple** option to create eight lines representing eight steps.
5. Explode the inner polyline.
6. Offset the right vertical line to the left using the through point method and the left endpoint of the upper-right horizontal line.
7. Offset the new line to the right using distance = 6".

8. The new shape of the plan should look like the following:

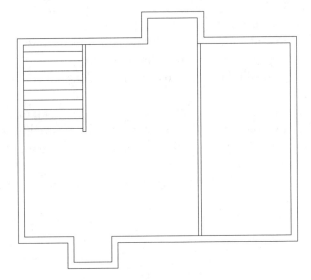

9. Save the file and close it.

4.3 THE FILLET COMMAND

- If you have the following:

- And you want them to look like this:

- Or, you want them to look like this:

- Then you need to use the **Fillet** command.
- Issue the **Fillet** command by selecting the first object and then the second object. It is a very simple AutoCAD command.
- The **Fillet** command works with two different settings:
  - Radius = 0 will create a neat intersection.
  - Radius > 0 will do the same except it will use an arc rather than a corner point.
- When you close the shape with an arc, what will happen to the original objects? To solve this issue, the **Fillet** command works in two different modes:
  - In **Trim** mode, the arc will be produced, and the original objects will be trimmed accordingly.
  - In **No trim** mode, the arc will be produced, but the original objects will stay intact.
- Here is an example:

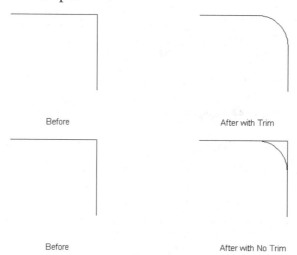

Before   After with Trim

Before   After with No Trim

- Make sure you are in the **Home** tab on the **Ribbon**, and, using the **Modify** panel, click the **Fillet** button.

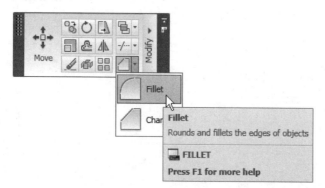

- The following prompt will appear:

```
Current settings: Mode = TRIM, Radius = 0.0000
Select first object or [Undo/Polyline/Radius/Trim/
Multiple]:
```

- The first line reports the current value of the mode and the radius.
- Choose between the different options: **Radius**, **Trim**, **Multiple**, and **Undo**.

Radius

- To set a new value for the radius, the following prompt will appear:

```
Specify fillet radius <0.0000>: (type in the new radius)
```

Trim

- To change the mode from **Trim** to **No trim,** or vice versa, the following prompt will appear:

```
Enter Trim mode option [Trim/No trim] <Trim>:(type t, or n)
```

Multiple

- By default, you can perform a single fillet per command by selecting the first object and the second object.
- If you want to perform multiple fillets in a single command, you have to select the **Multiple** mode first.

Undo

- You can use the **Undo** option while you are filleting to undo the last filleting action.
- NOTE ➤ When you fillet with a radius, the radius will be created in the current layer. Make sure that you are in the right layer.
- To end the command when you use the **Multiple** option, press [Enter] or right-click.
- Even if R > 0, you can still fillet with R = 0. To do so, simply hold the [Shift] key and click on the desired objects. Regardless of the current value of R, you will fillet with R = 0.
- You can use the **Fillet** command to fillet two parallel lines with an arc. AutoCAD will calculate the distance between the two lines, and take the radius to be one-half of this length.

FILLETING OBJECTS

Exercise 17
1. Start AutoCAD 2010.
2. Open the file *Exercise_17.dwg*.
3. Using the **Fillet** command, perform the following steps:
    a. Set the radius = 0.5.
    b. Set the mode = **Trim**.
4. Fillet the four edges to make the shape look like the following:

5. Using the **Fillet** command, perform the following steps:
    a. Mode = **No Trim**.
    b. Set **Fillet** to be **Multiple**.
6. Fillet the lines to get the following shape:

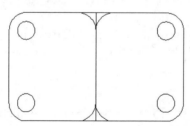

7. Save the file and close it.

4.4 THE CHAMFER COMMAND

- The **Chamfer** command is, in many ways, identical to the **Fillet** command, except that it creates a slanted edge rather than an arc.
- To create the slanted edge, we will use one of two methods:
    - Two distances
    - Length and angle

Two Distances

- There are three different examples of this method:
  - (Dist1 = Dist2) = 0.0, as in the following example:

Before   (Dist 1 = Dist 2) = 0

- (Dist1 = Dist2) > 0.0, as in the following example:

Before   (Dist 1 = Dist 2) > 0

- (Dist1 ≠ Dist2) > 0.0, as in the following example (regardless of which one will be selected first, Dist1 will be used):

Before   (Dist 1 ≠ Dist 2) > 0

Length and Angle

- To use this method, specify a length (which will be removed from the first object) and an angle, just as in the following example:

Before   Distance & Angle

- Make sure you are in the **Home** tab on the **Ribbon**, and, using the **Modify** panel, click the **Chamfer** button.

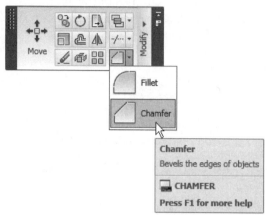

- The following prompt will appear:

```
(TRIM mode) Current chamfer Dist1 = 0.0000, Dist2 = 0.0000
Select first line or [Undo/Polyline/Distance/Angle /Trim/
Method/Multiple]:
```

- The first line reports the current mode and the distances (or length and angle).
- Choose between the different options: distances, angle, **Trim**, method, and **Multiple**.

Distances

- To set a new value for the distances, the following prompt will appear:

```
Specify first chamfer distance <0.0000>: (input the first distance)
Specify second chamfer distance <0.0000>: (input the second
distance)
```

Angle

- To set the new values for both the length and the angle, the following prompt will appear:

```
Specify chamfer length on the first line <0.0000>:
(input the length on first line)
Specify chamfer angle from the first line <0>:
(input the angle)
```

Trim

- To change the mode from **Trim** to **No trim**, or vice versa, the following prompt will appear:

```
Enter Trim mode option [Trim/No trim] <Trim>:
(type t, or n)
```

Method

- To specify the default method to be used in the **Chamfer** command, the following prompt will appear:

```
Enter trim method [Distance/Angle]
<Distance>: (type d, or a)
```

Multiple

- By default, you can perform a single chamfer per command by selecting the first object and the second object. If you want to perform multiple chamfers in a single command, you have to select the **Multiple** mode first.

 ■ When you chamfer, the slanted line will be created in the current layer. Make sure that you are in the right layer.

- To end the command when using the **Multiple** option, press [Enter] or right-click.
- The **Trim** or **No Trim** modes in the **Fillet** command will affect the **Chamfer** command and vice versa. If you change the mode in one of these two commands, the other command will reflect this change.

CHAMFERING OBJECTS

Exercise 18

1. Start AutoCAD 2010.
2. Open the file *Exercise_18.dwg*.
3. Using the **Chamfer** command, perform the following steps:
   a. Set Dist1 = 1.0.
   b. Set Dist2 = 0.4.
   c. Set the mode = **Trim**.
   d. Set the **Chamfer** command to **Multiple**.

4. Chamfer the four edges by selecting the proper line for the proper chamfering distance to make the shape look like the following:

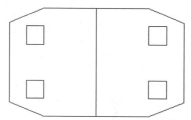

5. Using the **Chamfer** command, perform the following steps:
   a. Set the distance = 0.5.
   b. Set the angle = 30.
   c. Set the mode = **No trim**.
   d. Set the **Chamfer** command to **Multiple**.
6. Chamfer the inner line to make the shape look like the following:

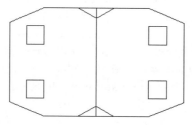

7. Save the file and close it.

■ The distance will be cut from the horizontal line and the angle will be cut from the vertical line.

4.5 THE TRIM COMMAND

■ Trimming means we want to remove part of an object by cutting the edge(s).
■ The **Trim** command is a two-step command:
   • The first step is to select the edge(s) to be cut. It can be one edge or as many as you wish.
   • The second step is to select the objects to be trimmed.

- The following example illustrates the trimming process:

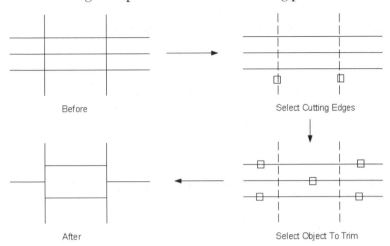

- Make sure you are in the **Home** tab on the **Ribbon**, and, using the **Modify** panel, click the **Trim** button.

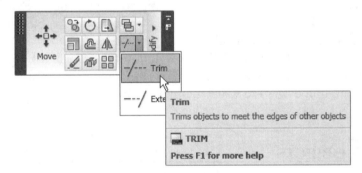

- The following prompt will appear:

```
Current settings: Projection=UCS, Edge=Extend
Select cutting edges ...
Select objects or <select all>:
```

- The first line displays the current settings.
- The second line tells you to select the cutting edges.
- Use any of the methods we learned in the **Erase** command. Once you are done, press [Enter] or right-click.
- You can also use the fastest method—the **select all** option—which will select all of the objects to act as cutting edges.
- The following prompt will appear:

```
Select object to trim or shift-select to extend or
[Fence/Crossing/Project/Edge/Erase/Undo]:
```

- Now, click on the parts you want to trim, one by one.
- If you made any mistakes, simply right-click to bring up the shortcut menu and select **Undo**, or type **u** in the **Command Window**.

Fence

- You can use the **Fence** option to speed up the selection process of objects to be trimmed. This can be done by specifying two or more points. A dotted line will be created and whatever objects it touches will be trimmed.

Crossing

- The same thing applies to the **Crossing** option. When you specify two opposite corners, a crossing window will appear and any object touched by the crossing will be trimmed.

Erase

- Sometimes, as a result of trimming, there will be some unwanted objects created. Instead of finishing the command and issuing an **Erase** command, AutoCAD makes this option available for you to erase objects while you are still in the **Trim** command.
- Type **r** in the **Command Window** and AutoCAD will ask you to select the objects you want to erase. Once you are done, press [Enter], and you will be prompted again to select another option.

TRIMMING OBJECTS

Exercise 19
1. Start AutoCAD 2010.
2. Open the file *Exercise_19.dwg*.
3. Using the **Trim** command, create the following two shapes:

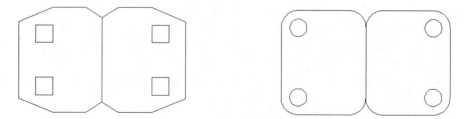

4. Save the file and close it.

- If you get a residual object you can use the **Erase** option in the **Trim** command to get rid of it.

4.6 THE EXTEND COMMAND

- The **Extend** command is the opposite of **Trim** command.
- When you use the **Extend** command, you will extend selected objects to the boundary edge(s).
- The **Extend** command is a two-step command:
  - The first step is to select the boundary edge(s). You can choose one edge or as many as you wish.
  - The second step is to select the objects to be extended.
- The following example illustrates the process of extending:

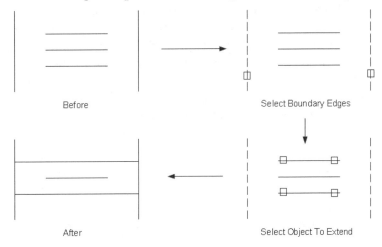

- Make sure you are in the **Home** tab on the **Ribbon**, and, using the **Modify** panel, click the **Extend** button.

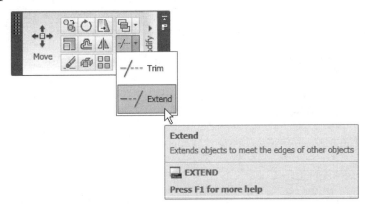

- The following prompt will appear:

```
Current settings: Projection=UCS, Edge=Extend
Select boundary edges ...
Select objects or <select all>:
```

- The first line displays the current settings.
- The second line tells you to select the boundary edges.
- Use any of the methods you know. Once you are done, press [Enter] or right-click.
- The following prompt will appear:

```
Select object to extend or shift-select to trim or
[Fence/Crossing/Project/Edge/Undo]:
```

- Now, click on the parts you want to extend, one by one.
- If you made a mistake, simply right-click to open the shortcut menu and select **Undo**, or type **u** in the **Command Window**.
- The rest of the options are the same as the **Trim** command.
- NOTE ➤ While you are in the **Trim** command, and while you are clicking on the objects to be trimmed, if you hold the [Shift] key and click, you will extend the objects rather than trim them. See the following example:

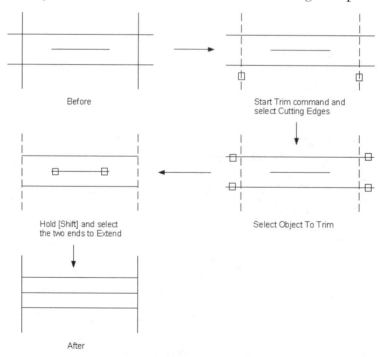

Before

Start Trim command and
select Cutting Edges

Hold [Shift] and select
the two ends to Extend

Select Object To Trim

After

EXTENDING OBJECTS

 Exercise 20

1. Start AutoCAD 2010.
2. Open the file *Exercise_20.dwg*.
3. Using the **Extend** and **Trim** commands, create the following shape:

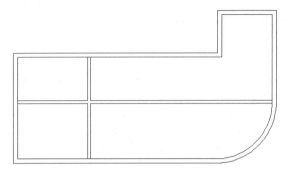

4. Save the file and close it.

4.7 THE LENGTHEN COMMAND

- With the **Extend** command, we needed an object to serve as a boundary in order to extend the rest of the objects to it.
- The **Lengthen** (or shorten, as it serves both purposes) command will do this without a boundary.
- Make sure you are in the **Home** tab on the **Ribbon**, and, after extending the **Modify** panel, select the **Lengthen** button.

- The following prompt will appear:

```
Select an object or [Delta/Percent/Total/Dynamic]:
```

- If you click on any object, it will give you the current length.
- The command will do the lengthening (or shortening) using **Delta**, **Percent**, **Total**, or **Dynamic**.

Delta

- This command is used if you want to add or remove extra length to or from the current length.
- If you input a negative value, the **Lengthen** command will shorten the line.
- The following prompt will appear:

```
Enter delta length or [Angle] <0.0000>: (input the
extra length to be added)
```

Percent

- If you want to add to or remove from the length, specify a percentage of the current length.
- The number should be positive, and a nonzero number. If it was > 100, it will lengthen. If it was < 100, it will shorten.
- The following prompt will appear:

```
Enter percentage length <100.0000>: (input the new
percentage)
```

Total

- Use the **Total** option if you want the new total length of the line to be equal to the number you will input.
- If the new number is greater than the current length, the line will lengthen. If the new number is less than the current length, the line will shorten.
- The following prompt will appear:

```
Specify total length or [Angle] <1.0000)>: (input
the new total length)
```

Dynamic

- This option is used to specify a new length of the object, using the dynamic move of the mouse.
- The following prompt will appear:

```
Select an object to change or [Undo]: (select the desired
object)
Specify new endpoint: (move the mouse, up until you reach to
the desired length)
```

- You can use only one method per command.

LENGTHENING OBJECTS

Exercise 21

1. Start AutoCAD 2010.
2. Open the file *Exercise_21.dwg*.
3. Using the **Lengthen** command and the **Delta** option, shorten the two vertical lines by 1 unit.
4. Using the **Lengthen** command and the **Total** option, make the total length of the two horizontal lines = 5.
5. As you can see, the lower line did not come to the end like the upper line.
6. Using the **Lengthen** command and the **Percent** option, set percent = 104, and select the end of the line.
7. The output should look like the following:

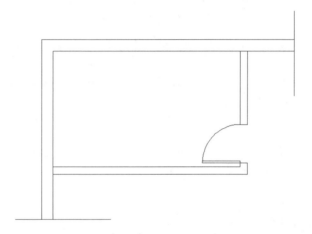

8. Save the file and close it.

4.8 THE JOIN COMMAND

-   While you are modifying your drawing you may end up with a line broken into segments, which will need to join into one single line. The same thing may happen with arcs.
-   If you have a polyline, you can join other objects to it, such as lines and arcs.
-   Make sure you are in the **Home** tab on the **Ribbon**, and, by extending the **Modify** panel, select the **Lengthen** button.

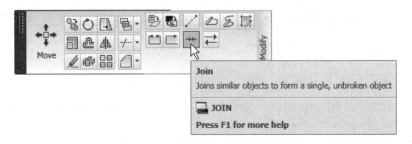

- AutoCAD will show the following prompts:

```
Select source object:
Select lines to join to source: (Select the source
object) Select lines to join to source: (Depending on the
source object, the following prompt will ask to
select the objects to join, once you are done
press [Enter]) 1 line joined to source
```

- If you select a line object, the other lines should be collinear; gaps are allowed.
- If you select an arc object, the other arcs should be part of the same imaginary circle; gaps are allowed.
- There is a special prompt in the **Arc** option to close the arc and formulate a circle.
- You can join a polyline to any other objects (lines, arcs, etc.) but, in this case, no gaps are allowed.

JOINING OBJECTS

 Exercise 22
1. Start AutoCAD 2010.
2. Open the file *Exercise_22.dwg*.
3. This file displays what you might find after recovering a corrupt file.
4. You will find broken lines, arcs, and polylines.
5. Using the **Join** command, make the arc a full circle.
6. Using the **Join** command, connect the two broken lines.
7. Join all of the lines to the polyline.
8. Save the file and close it.

DRAWING THE PLAN (METRIC)

Workshop 2-A

1. Start AutoCAD 2010 and open the file *Workshop_02.dwg*.
2. Make the layer **Walls** current.
3. Using the **Pline** command, draw the outer lines first (without the dimension) starting from point 8000,3000 using all the methods you learned in Chapter 2.

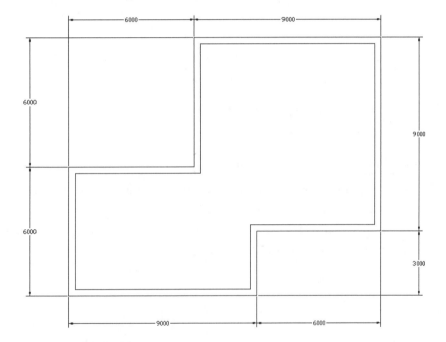

4. Using the **Offset** command, offset the polyline to the inside with an offset distance = 300.
5. Explode the inner polyline.
6. Using the **Offset**, **Fillet**, **Chamfer**, **Trim**, **Extend**, **Lengthen**, and **Zoom** commands, create the interior walls using the following dimensions:

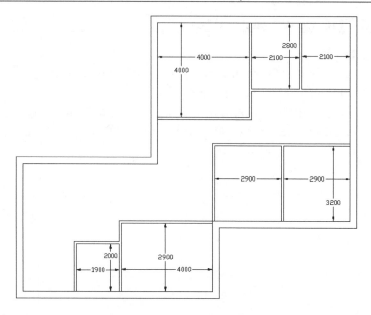

■ The thickness of all inner walls = 100.

7. Make the door openings, taking the following into consideration:

   a. All door openings = 900.

   b. Always take 100 clear distances from the walls for the door openings (except for the outside door take 500).

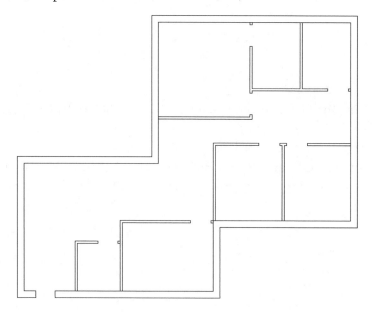

■ To make the door openings, use the following technique:
- Offset an existing wall (say, 100 for internal doors).
- Offset the new line (say, 900 for room doors).
- You will have the following shape:

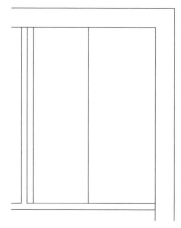

- Extend the two vertical lines to the lower horizontal line as shown in the following:

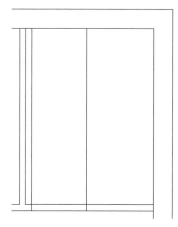

- Using the **Trim** command, select all horizontal and vertical lines as cutting edges, then press [Enter]. Trim the unnecessary parts by clicking on the objects (you can use **Crossing**, which is faster).

- This is what you will get:

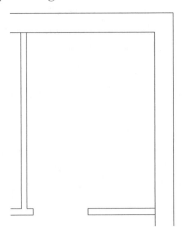

8. Save the file and close it.

DRAWING THE PLAN (IMPERIAL)

Workshop 2-B

1. Start AutoCAD 2010 and open the file *Workshop_02.dwg*.
2. Make the layer **Walls** current.
3. Using the **Pline** command, draw the outer lines (without the dimensions) starting from point 16',10' using all the methods you learned in Chapter 2.

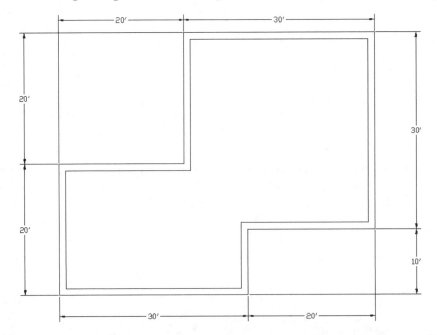

4. Using the **Offset** command, offset the polyline to the inside with an offset distance = 1'.

5. Explode the inner polyline.

6. Using the **Offset**, **Fillet**, **Chamfer**, **Trim**, **Extend**, **Lengthen**, and **Zoom** commands, create the interior walls using the following dimensions:

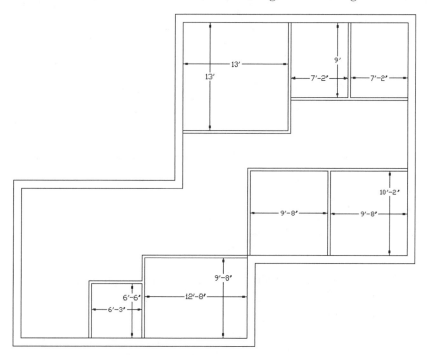

- The thickness of all inner walls = 4".

7. Make the door openings, taking the following into consideration:

   a. All door openings = 3'.

   b. Always take 4" clear distance from the walls for the door openings (except for the outside door take 1'6").

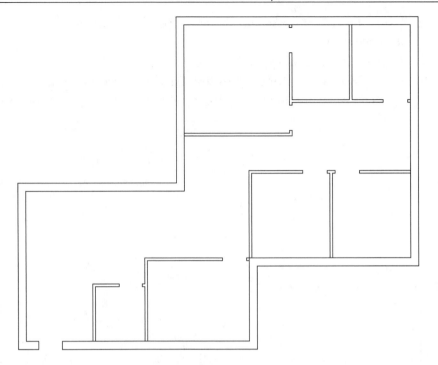

 ■ To make the door openings, use the following technique:
- Offset an existing wall (say, 4" for internal doors).
- Offset the new line (say, 3' for room door).
- You will have the following shape:

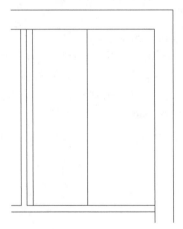

- Extend the two vertical lines to the lower horizontal line as shown in the following:

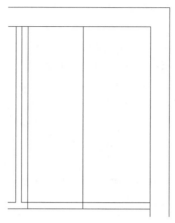

- Using the **Trim** command, select all horizontal and vertical lines as cutting edges, then press [Enter]. Trim the unnecessary parts by clicking on the objects (you can use **Crossing**, which is faster).
- This is what you will get:

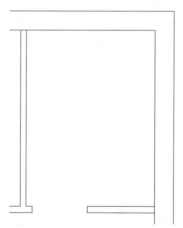

8. Save the file and close it

CHAPTER REVIEW

1. You can use more than one offset distance within the same **Offset** command.
   a. True, two offset distances can be used.
   b. True, you can use as many as you wish.
   c. False, only one offset distance can be used.
   d. The only method available in the **Offset** command is the through point method.

2. In the **Lengthen** command, using the **Percent** option, 150% should be input as _____.

3. While you are trimming, you can extend, and vice versa.
   a. True
   b. False

4. You can fillet using an arc, but you need to specify:
   a. Distances
   b. Radius
   c. Radius and distances
   d. Length and angle

5. There are two methods to chamfer: Distances, and Length and Angle.
   a. True
   b. False

6. The first step in the **Extend** command is to select _____, and the second step is to select_____.

7. If you want to join lines, they should be _____, and _____ are allowed.

CHAPTER REVIEW ANSWERS

1. c
2. 150
3. a
4. b
5. a
6. Boundary Edge(s), Objects to extend
7. collinear, gaps

Chapter **5** MODIFYING COMMANDS

In This Chapter

5.1 INTRODUCTION

- In this chapter, we will learn the core of the modifying commands in AutoCAD®.
- We will cover nine commands, which will enable you to make any type of changes in a drawing.
- First, we will discuss the selection process (more in depth than what we discussed in Chapter 2).
- Then, we will discuss the following commands:
  - The **Move** command moves objects from one place to another.
  - The **Copy** command copies objects.
  - The **Rotate** command turns objects using rotation angles.
  - The **Scale** command creates larger or smaller objects using a scale factor.

- The **Array** command creates copies of objects in a matrix, circular, or semicircular fashion.
- The **Mirror** command creates mirror images of selected objects.
- The **Stretch** command either increases or decreases the length of objects.
- The **Break** command breaks an object into two pieces.

- We will wrap up with a discussion of **Grips** in AutoCAD.

5.2 SELECTING OBJECTS

- All of the modifying commands (with some exceptions) will ask you the same question:

```
Select objects:
```

- In Chapter 2, we looked at some of the methods used to select objects. We will now expand our knowledge in this area.
- All of the methods we discuss will involve typing at least one letter in the **Command Window** at the **Select objects** prompt.

W (Window)

- If you typed **W**, the **Window** mode will be available whether you moved to the right or to the left.

C (Crossing)

- If you typed **C**, the **Crossing** mode will be available whether you moved to the right or to the left.

WP (Window Polygon)

- If you want to select multiple objects without the constraint of the rectangle window, you can use the **Window Polygon** mode.
- When you type **WP** and press [Enter], the following prompt will appear:

```
First polygon point: (specify the first point of the polygon)
Specify endpoint of line or [Undo]: (specifying the second
point)
Specify endpoint of line or [Undo]: (specify the third
point, etc.)
```

- When you are done, press [Enter] to end the **WP** mode.

- The objects that are fully inside the **Window Polygon** will be selected. If any part (even a small part) is outside the shape, it will not be selected. See the following example:

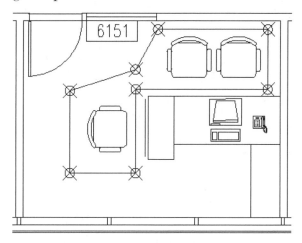

CP (Crossing Polygon)

- The **Crossing Polygon** mode is the same as the **Window Polygon** mode, except it has the features of the **Crossing** mode. That means that whatever it fully contains—plus any object that touches it—will be selected.

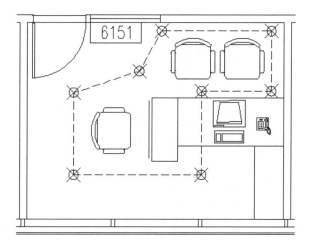

F (Fence)

- The main function of the **Fence** mode is to touch objects.
- The **Fence** mode was discussed when we introduced the **Trim** and **Extend** modes.

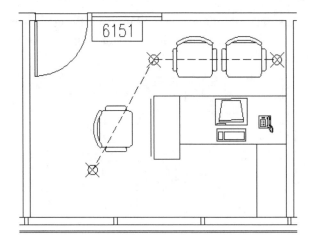

L (Last)

- The **Last** mode is used to select the last object drawn.

P (Previous)

- The **Previous** mode is used to select the last selection set used.

All

- To select all objects in the current file use **All**.

Deselect

- If you select a group of objects, then you discover that one or two of the objects were selected by mistake. How do you deselect them?
- Simply hold the [Shift] key, click these objects, and they will be deselected.

Other Methods for Selecting Objects

- There are other methods used to select objects that will make your life easier.
- There is a good technique called the **Noun/Verb selection**, which will allow the user to select an object first and then issue the command.
- The cursor looks like the following:

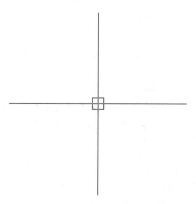

- As you can see, there is a pick box inside the cursor.
- Without issuing any command, you can:
  - Click on any object to select it.
  - Find an empty space, click, and then go to the right to get the **Window** mode.
  - Find an empty space, click, and then go to the left to get the **Crossing** mode.
- Once you select the desired objects, right-click to get the following shortcut menu:

- From this shortcut menu, you can access five modifying commands without typing a single letter on the keyboard or issuing any commands from the menus or the toolbars. These commands are: **Erase**, **Move**, **Copy Selection**, **Scale**, and **Rotate**.
- Make sure that the **Noun/Verb selection** mode is turned on using the **Menu Browser** by selecting **Tools/Options**, then the **Selection** tab, and under **Selection modes**, click the **Noun/Verb selection** checkbox to turn it on (that is, if it was off).

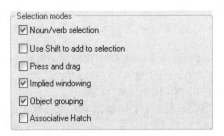

 ■ This technique will not work with the **Offset**, **Fillet**, **Chamfer**, **Trim**, **Extend**, or **Lengthen** commands. It will work with the **Join** command.

5.3 THE MOVE COMMAND

- The **Move** command is used to move objects from one place to another.
- Make sure you are in the **Home** tab on the **Ribbon**, and, using the **Modify** panel, select the **Move** button.

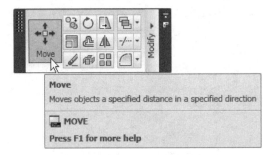

- The **Move** command is a three-step command.
- The first step is to:

```
Select objects:
```

- Once you are done, press [Enter] or right-click.

■ The next prompt will ask you to:

```
Specify base point or [Displacement]
<Displacement>: (Specify the base point)
```

■ The *base point* will be used in four other commands. What is a base point?
  • The simplest way to define a base point is to call it a *handle* point.
  • There is no golden rule that defines a right point as a base point.
  • Rather, you have to take it case by case, so it may be the center of a group of objects or it may be in the upper left-hand corner.
  • This is also true for commands like **Move**, **Copy**, and **Stretch**. But for a command such as **Rotate**, the base point is the point where the whole shape will rotate around. In the **Scale** command, it will be the point that the whole shape will shrink or enlarge relative to it.
■ The third prompt will be:

```
Specify second point or <use first point as
displacement>: (Specify the second point)
```

■ The command will end automatically.
■ See the following example:

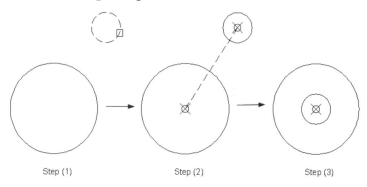

Step (1)   Step (2)   Step (3)

MOVING OBJECTS

Exercise 23
1. Start AutoCAD 2010.
2. Open the file *Exercise_23.dwg*.
3. Move the four objects (bathtub, toilet, sink, and door) to their respective places to make the bathroom look like the following:

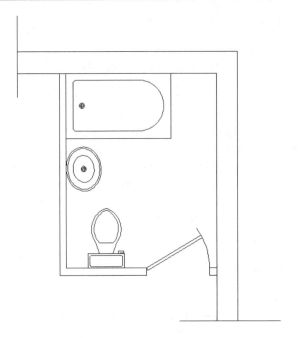

4. Save the file and close it.

- For the toilet, use the midpoint of the inside wall.
- For the sink, use the left quadrant and the midpoint of the inside wall.

5.4 THE COPY COMMAND

- The **Copy** command is used to copy objects.
- Make sure you are in the **Home** tab on the **Ribbon**, and, using the **Modify** panel, select the **Copy** button.

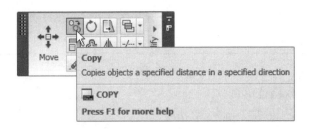

- The **Copy** command is a three-step command.
- The first step is to:

```
Select objects:
```

- Once you are done, press [Enter] or right-click.
- The next prompt will ask you to:

```
Specify base point or [Displacement] <Displacement>:
```
(Specify the base point)

- The third prompt will be to:

```
Specify second point or [Exit/Undo] <Exit>: (Specify the
second point)
Specify second point or [Exit/Undo] <Exit>: (Specify
another second point)
```

- Once you are done, press [Enter] or right-click.
- If you made a mistake, simply type **u** into the **Command Window** to undo the last action.
- See the following example:

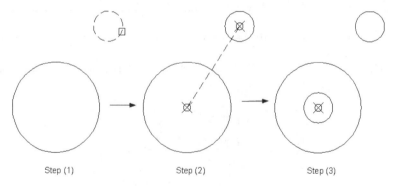

| Step (1) | Step (2) | Step (3) |

COPYING OBJECTS

Exercise 24

1. Start AutoCAD 2010.
2. Open the file *Exercise_24.dwg*.
3. Copy the chair three times to make the room look like the following:

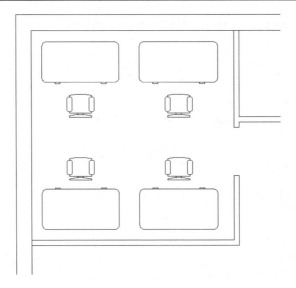

4. Save the file and close it.

- Use **Polar Tracking**, **OSNAP**, and **OTRACK** to make sure they are aligned.

5.5 THE ROTATE COMMAND

- The **Rotate** command is used to rotate objects around a point using a rotation angle.
- Make sure you are in the **Home** tab on the **Ribbon**, and, using the **Modify** panel, select the **Rotate** button.

- The **Rotate** command is a three-step command.
- The first step is to:

```
Select objects:
```

- Once you are done, press [Enter] or right-click.
- The next prompt will ask you to:

```
Specify base point: (Specify the base point)
```

- The third prompt will be to:

```
Specify rotation angle or [Copy/Reference] <0>:
```
(specify the rotation angle, -=CW, +=CCW)

- You can use the **Copy** option if you want to rotate a copy of the objects selected while keeping the original intact.
- The command will end automatically.
- See the following example:

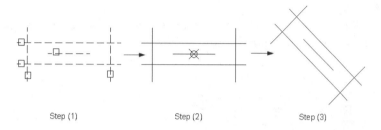

Step (1)   Step (2)   Step (3)

ROTATING OBJECTS

Exercise 25

1. Start AutoCAD 2010.
2. Open the file *Exercise_25.dwg*.
3. Rotate the two chairs (each using a different command) around the center of each chair to make the room look like the following:

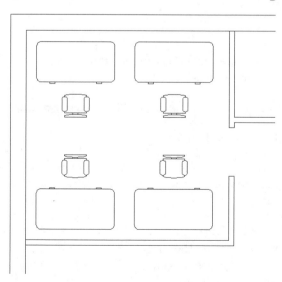

4. Save the file and close it.

- The best way to do this exercise is to use either **Polar Tracking** or type the angles. You may need to move some things around to make the room look perfect.

5.6 THE SCALE COMMAND

- The **Scale** Command is used to enlarge or shrink objects using a scale factor.
- Make sure you are in the **Home** tab on the **Ribbon**, and, using the **Modify** panel, select the **Scale** button.

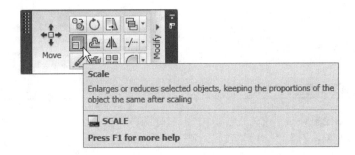

- The **Scale** command is a three-step command.
- The first step is to:

```
Select objects:
```

- Once you are done, press [Enter] or right-click.
- The next prompt will ask you to:

```
Specify base point: (Specify the base point)
```

- The third prompt will be to:

```
Specify scale factor or [Copy/Reference] <1.0000>:
(specify the scale factor, the number should be a non-zero
positive number)
```

- You can use the **Copy** option if you want to scale a copy of the objects selected while keeping the original intact.
- The command will end automatically.
- See the following example:

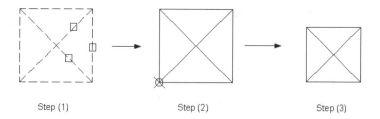

Step (1)   Step (2)   Step (3)

SCALING OBJECTS

Exercise 26

1. Start AutoCAD 2010.
2. Open the file *Exercise_26.dwg*.
3. Set the scale factor = 0.8 to scale the bathtub using the upper left-hand corner as the base point.
4. Set the scale factor = 1.2 to scale the sink using the quadrant on the left side as the base point.
5. The room should look like the following:

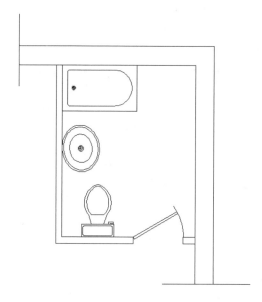

6. Save the file and close it.

5.7 THE ARRAY COMMAND

- The **Array** command is used to create duplicates of objects using two methods:
  - Rectangular array (matrix shape)
  - Polar array (circular or semi circular shape)
- Make sure you are in the **Home** tab on the **Ribbon**, and, using the **Modify** panel, select the **Array** button.

Rectangular

- If you want to create a duplicate of objects simulating the matrix shape, you should select the **Rectangular Array**.
- The following dialog box will appear:

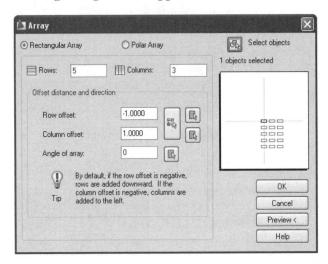

- First, click the **Select Objects** button to select the desired objects. Once you are done, press [Enter] or right-click.

- Next, specify the number of **Rows** and the number of **Columns** (the original object is inclusive).
- Specify the **Row offset** (the distance between rows), and specify the **Column offset** (the distance between columns). While you are doing this keep two things in mind:
  - You have to be consistent. Measure the distance from the same reference point (e.g., top-to-top, bottom-to-bottom, center-to-center, etc.).
  - You have to take note of the direction in which you are copying. If you input a positive number, it will be either to the right or up. If you input a negative number, it will be either to the left or down.
- Specify the **Angle of array**. By default, it will repeat the objects using the orthogonal angles.
- Click the **Preview** button to see the result of your input.
- AutoCAD will display the result and the following prompt will appear:

```
Pick or press Esc to return to dialog or <Right-click to
accept array>:
```

- If you like the result, press [Enter] or right-click.
- If not, press [Esc].
- See the following example:

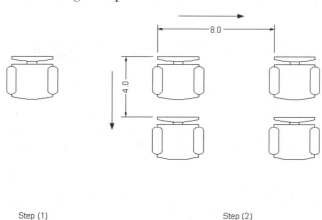

Step (1)   Step (2)

RECTANGULAR ARRAY

Exercise 27

1. Start AutoCAD 2010.
2. Open the file *Exercise_27.dwg*.
3. Using the **Rectangular Array**, array the chairs to look like the following:

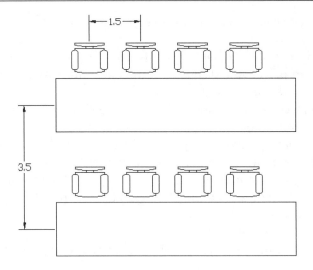

4.   Save the file and close it.

The **Polar Array** Command

- The **Polar Array** command is used if you want to duplicate certain objects simulating circular or semicircular shapes.
- The following dialog box will appear:

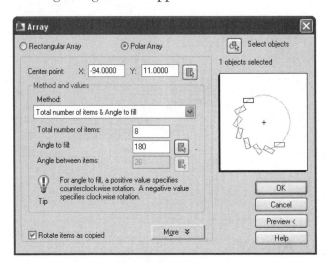

- First, click the **Select Objects** button to select the desired objects. Once you are done, press [Enter] or right-click.

- Next, specify the **Center point** of the array, either by inputting the coordinates in X and Y, or by clicking the **Pick Center Point** button and specifying the point by using the mouse.
- You have three pieces of data to input and AutoCAD will only take two of them. These are:
  - Total number of items
  - Angle to fill
  - Angle between items
- The following diagram illustrates the relationship between the three parameters:

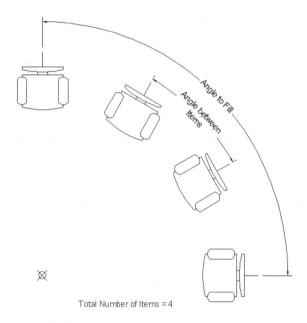

Total Number of Items = 4

- You can specify two out of three parameters, which gives you three different methods. They are:
  - Method 1: Specify the total number of items and the angle to fill. AutoCAD will figure out the angles between the items.
  - Method 2: Specify the total number of items and the angle between the items. AutoCAD will know the angle to fill.
  - Method 3: Specify the angle to fill and the angle between the items, and AutoCAD will calculate the total number of items.
- Under **Methods and values**, select the proper method and input the corresponding values.
- Specify whether or not you want to **Rotate items as copied**. See the following example:

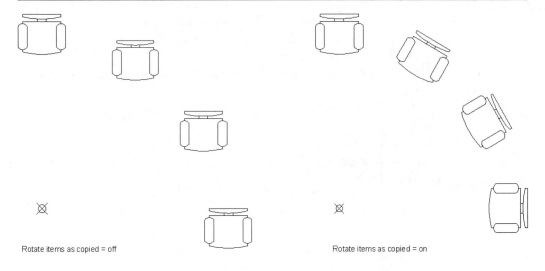

Rotate items as copied = off   Rotate items as copied = on

POLAR ARRAY

Exercise 28

1. Start AutoCAD 2010.

2. Open the file *Exercise_28.dwg*.

3. Using the **Polar Array** command, array the square so you will get the following result:

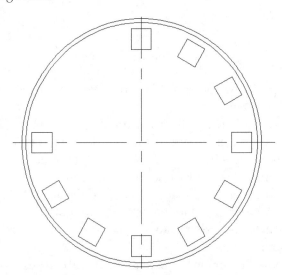

4. Save the file and close it.

5.8 THE MIRROR COMMAND

- The **Mirror** command is used to create a mirror image of selected objects.
- Make sure you are in the **Home** tab on the **Ribbon**, and, using the **Modify** panel, select the **Mirror** button.

- The first step is to:

```
Select objects:
```

- Once you are done, press [Enter] or right-click.
- Now, you need to specify the mirror line by specifying two points:

```
Specify first point of mirror line: (specify the first point
of the mirror line)
Specify second point of mirror line: (specify the second
point of the mirror line)
```

- The following applies to the mirror line:
  - There is no need to draw a line to act as a mirror line; two points will do the job.
  - The length of the mirror is not important, but the location and angle of the mirror line will affect the final result.
- The last prompt will be:

```
Erase source objects? [Yes/No] <N>: (type N, or Y)
```

- The **Mirror** command will produce an image in all cases, but what should AutoCAD do with the source objects? You can keep them or erase them.
- The **Mirror** command ends automatically.
- NOTE If part of the objects to be mirrored is text, you have to control whether you want to treat it as any other object and mirror it, or simply copy it.
- To do that, prior to issuing the **Mirror** command, type **mirrtext** in the **Command Window** and the following prompt will appear:

```
Enter new value for MIRRTEXT <0>:
```

- If you input 0 (zero), then the text will be copied.
- If you input 1, then the text will be mirrored.
- See the following example:

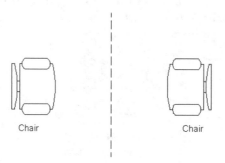

Chair   Chair

Mirrtext = 0 & Erase Source Objects = No

MIRRORING OBJECTS

 Exercise 29

1. Start AutoCAD 2010.
2. Open the file *Exercise_29.dwg*.
3. Using the **Mirror** command, create the following shape:

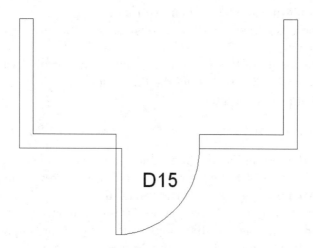

D15

4. Save the file and close it.

5.9 THE STRETCH COMMAND

- The **Stretch** command is used to increase or decrease the length of selected objects.
- Make sure you are in the **Home** tab on the **Ribbon**, and, using the **Modify** panel, select the **Stretch** button.

- The first step is to:

```
Select objects to stretch by crossing-window
or crossing-polygon...
```

- The **Stretch** command is one of the few commands that insists on a certain method of selection.
- The **Stretch** command asks users to select using either **C** or **CP**.
- As we discussed previously, **C** and **CP** will select any object contained inside and any object touched (crossed) by **C** or **CP** lines.
- The **Stretch** command will utilize both facilities by setting the following rules:
  - Any object contained fully inside **C** or **CP** will be moved.
  - Any object crossed by **C** or **CP** will be stretched.
- Once you are done, press [Enter] or right-click.
- The second prompt will be to:

```
Specify base point or [Displacement]
<Displacement>: (specify Base point)
```

- The third prompt will be to:

```
Specify second point or <use first point as displacement>:
(specify the destination point)
```

- The **Stretch** command ends automatically.

- See the following example:

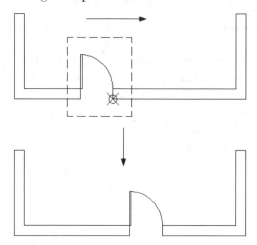

STRETCHING OBJECTS

 Exercise 30

1. Start AutoCAD 2010.
2. Open the file *Exercise_30.dwg*.
3. Using the **Stretch** command, stretch the door 2 units to the left so it will look like the following:

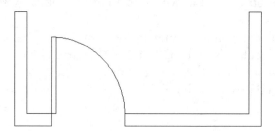

4. Save the file and close it.

5.10 THE BREAK COMMAND

- The **Break** command is used to break an object into two pieces.
- Make sure you are in the **Home** tab on the **Ribbon**, and, by using the **Modify** panel, expand it and select the **Break** button.

- The first step is to:

`Select object:`

- You can break one object at a time. When you select this object, AutoCAD will prompt you with the following:

`Specify second break point or [First point]:`

- To understand this prompt, take note of the following points:
  - In order to break an object you have to specify two points on it.
  - The selection you make can be considered either a selection and a first point or a selection only. If you consider the selection as a selection and first point, respond to this prompt by specifying the second point.
  - If you want the selection to only be the selection, type the letter **F** in the **Command Window** and AutoCAD will respond with the following prompt:

`Specify first break point:` ***(specify first breaking point)***

`Specify second break point:` ***(specify second breaking point)***

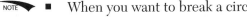
- When you want to break a circle, take care to specify the two points CCW.
- See the following example:

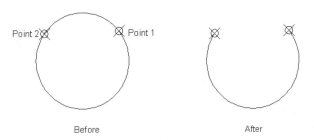

- There is another tool called **Break at Point** in the **Modify** panel on the **Home** tab.

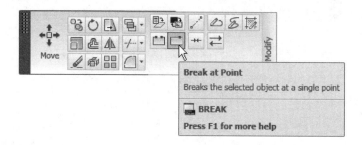

- This is similar to the **Break** command except for the following differences:
    - You will be asked to select only one point.
    - AutoCAD will assume that the first point and the second point are in the same place.
    - The object will be broken into two objects but connected.

BREAKING OBJECTS

Exercise 31

1.   Start AutoCAD 2010.
2.   Open the file *Exercise_31.dwg*.
3.   Using the **Break** command, break the two circles to look something like this:

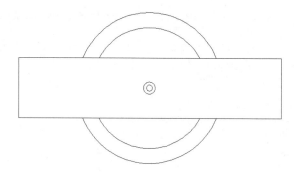

4.   Save the file and close it.

5.11 GRIPS

Introduction

- **Grips** is a method of modifying your objects easily and quickly.
- **Grips** is done with a simple click on an object, or multiple objects, without issuing any commands.
- **Grips** will do two things for you:
  - It will select the objects, and they will be ready for any modifying command to be issued, as they will act as a selection set.
  - Blue (default color) squares will appear at certain places depending on the type of the object. Here are some examples:

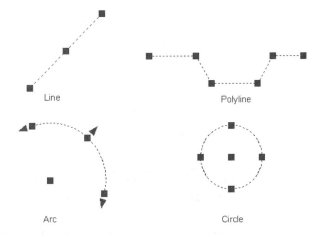

- These squares are the grips.
- There is a magnet relationship between these squares and the pick box of the crosshairs.
- Also, if you hover over grips, the blue will turn to green, indicating the current grip.
- If you click on one of these blue squares, you will:
  - Make it hot, turning it to red
  - Make this grip a base point
  - Start a group of five **Modify** commands (using the right-click)

The Five Commands

- Once you make one of the blue squares hot (by clicking on it), this grip will become the base point for five commands, they are:
  - **Move**
  - **Mirror**

- **Rotate**
- **Scale**
- **Stretch**

■ To see these commands, right-click and the following shortcut menu will appear:

■ The other options available in the shortcut menu are:
- **Base Point**, which is used to define a new base point other than the one you started with.
- **Copy**, which is a mode rather than a command. **Copy** mode works with the other five commands and will give you the ability to **Rotate with Copy**, **Scale with Copy**, etc.

Steps

■ The steps to use **Grips** are as follows:
- Select the object(s) desired (direct clicking, **Window** mode, or **Crossing** mode).
- Select one of the grips to be your base point and click it. It will become hot (red by default).
- Right-click and select the desired command from the shortcut menu. You can now specify another base point and/or you can select the **Copy** mode.
- Perform the steps of the desired command.
- Once you are done, press [Esc] either once or twice depending on the command you are working with.

■ You can use **OSNAP** with **Grips** with no limitations. Also, you can use **Polar Tracking** and **OTRACK**, so the modification will be accurate.
■ **Mirror** is the only command that does not explicitly ask for a base point. Why is it listed with the other four commands? The answer is that AutoCAD considers the first point of the mirror line to be the base point.
■ In order to keep both the original and the mirrored image using **Grips**, you have to select the **Copy** mode after you select the **Mirror** command.
■ You can deselect certain objects from the grips by holding the [Shift] key and clicking on the object, avoiding the blue squares.

Dynamic Input

■ **Dynamic Input** can give you information about the objects with their grips appearing on the screen.
■ If you hover over an end grip of a line, **Dynamic Input** tells you the length and the angle of that line.

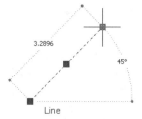

■ If you hover over an end grip shared between two lines, **Dynamic Input** tells you the length and angle of both lines:

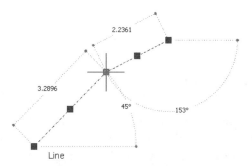

■ If you hover over the middle grip of an arc, **Dynamic Input** tells you the radius and the included angle of the arc:

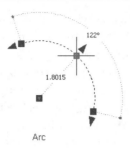

Arc

- If you hover over the quadrant grip of the circle, **Dynamic Input** tells you the radius of the circle:

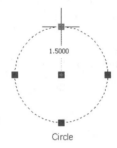

Circle

- If you hover over an intermediate grip of a polyline, **Dynamic Input** tells you the lengths of the line segments (without the angles):

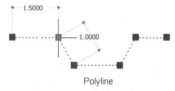

Polyline

USING GRIPS

 Exercise 32
1.   Start AutoCAD 2010.
2.   Open the file *Exercise_32.dwg*.
3.   Without issuing any commands, select the upper circle. Make the center hot, then right-click and select **Scale**, then right-click again and select **Copy**. At the **Scale factor** prompt type **0.5**. Press [Esc] twice.
4.   In the right part of the base, without issuing any commands, select the rectangle. Make one of the blue grips hot by clicking it, right-click, select **Rotate**, then right-click again and select **Base Point**. Specify a new base point, which is the center of the rectangle (using **OSNAP** and **OTRACK**), and setting the Rotation angle = 90. Press [Esc] twice.

5. Select the rotated rectangle at the right part of the base, select any grip to make it hot, then right-click and select **Mirror**. Right-click again and select **Copy**. Right-click for a third time and select **Base Point**. Specify one of the two endpoints of the vertical lines separating the two parts of the base and then specify the other endpoint. Press [Esc] twice. The shape will look like this:

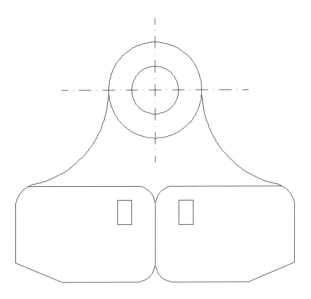

6. Save the file and close it.

CHAPTER REVIEW

1. What do the commands **Move**, **Copy**, **Rotate**, **Scale**, and **Stretch** have in common?
   a. They are all modifying commands.
   b. They all use the base point concept.
   c. They all change the length of an object.
   d. A and B.
2. In the **Stretch** command, you have to use _____ or _____ while selecting objects.
3. **Mirrtext** is used to control whether to copy or mirror the text in the **Mirror** command.
   a. True
   b. False

4. If you break a circle, take care to specify the two points:
   a. CCW
   b. CW
   c. It doesn't matter
   d. You can't break a circle
5. You can scale using a Scale factor = –1.
   a. True
   b. False
6. In the **Array** command and the **Rectangular** option, the **Row offset** must be _____ if you want to repeat the objects downward.

CHAPTER REVIEW ANSWERS

1. d
2. **C** or **CP**
3. a
4. a
5. b
6. negative

Chapter **6** **DEALING WITH BLOCKS**

6.1 WHAT ARE BLOCKS?

- A block in AutoCAD® is any shape that is repeated in one or more drawings more than once.
- Instead of drawing it each and every time you need it, use the following steps:
  - Draw it once.
  - Store it as a block.
  - Insert it as many times as you wish.
- Blocks in AutoCAD have changed over the years, which has made some of the old procedures obsolete.
- In this chapter, we will discuss the old methods, but we will concentrate more on the new methods of using blocks.

6.2 CREATING BLOCKS

- The first step in creating blocks in AutoCAD is to draw the desired shape.
- While drawing the shape, consider the following three guidelines:
  - Draw the shape in Layer 0 (zero).
  - Draw the shape in certain units.
  - Draw the shape in the right dimensions.

Why Layer 0?

- Layer 0 is different from any other layer in AutoCAD, because it will allow the block to be transparent both in color and in linetype.
- If you draw the shape that will be a block while layer 0 is current, then insert it into another layer with red color and dashdot linetype so the block will be red and dashdot.

Why Certain Units?

- If you want AutoCAD to automatically rescale your block to fit into the current drawing units, you have to specify the units of the block.

What Are the Right Dimensions?

- Right dimensions are either:
  - The real dimensions of the shape.
  - Values for the distances, such as 1, 10, 100, 1000. It will be easier to scale the block once you insert it.
- Let's assume we draw the following shape:

- The next step would be to think about a point that will act as the base point (the handle for this block).
- Also, think of a good name for this block.
- With all of these in mind, you can now issue the command.

- Make sure you are in the **Home** tab on the **Ribbon**, and, by using the **Block** panel, select the **Create** button:

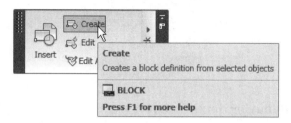

- The following dialog box will appear:

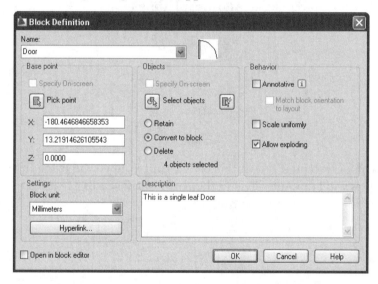

- Type the name of the block (similar to the layer naming conditions, it should not exceed 255 characters).
- Under **Base point**, click the **Pick point** button to input the base point of the block. Once you are done, press [Enter] or right-click. Or, you can select the checkbox **Specify On-screen** to specify the base point after the dialog box is closed.
- Under **Objects**, click the **Select objects** button to select the objects. Once you are done, press [Enter] or right-click. Or, you can select the checkbox **Specify On-screen** to specify the base point after the dialog box is closed.
- To decide what to do with the objects you draw to create this block, select one of the following three choices:
  - Retain
  - Convert to block
  - Delete

- Under **Behavior**, set the following:
  - Leave **Annotative** off (this is an advanced feature).
  - Choose to **Scale uniformly** (X-scale = Y-scale) or not.
  - Choose whether to **Allow exploding** or not.

- Under **Settings**, select the **Block unit** you will be using in your drawing. This will help AutoCAD in the **Automatic scaling** feature.

- Click the **Hyperlink** button and the following dialog box will appear:

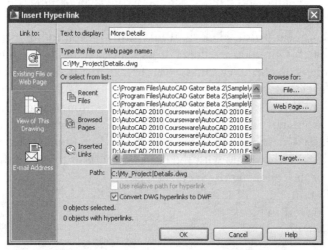

- This dialog box will allow users to insert a hyperlink inside the block to take them to a website, a drawing file with more details, an MS Word file, an Excel file for calculation, etc.
- After you finish, when you approach the block, you will see something like the following:

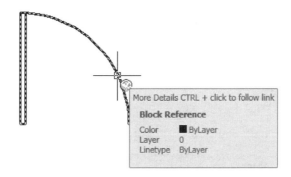

- As you can see, the shape of the hyperlink will be displayed and a help message will appear telling you to hold the [Ctrl] key and click the block to open the desired link.
- Write any description for your block.
- Select whether to allow this block to be opened in the block editor (block editor is an advanced feature used to create dynamic blocks) or to keep it off for the time being.
- When you are done, click **OK**.
- Now, let's imagine that our drawing has a cabinet, the door of the cabinet will be opened, and the defined block will be put inside it. This block will be intact. Even when you insert it, you will only insert a copy of it.
- You can define as many blocks as you wish.

CREATING A BLOCK (METRIC)

 Workshop 3-A

1. Start AutoCAD 2010.
2. Open the file *Workshop_03.dwg*.
3. Make layer 0 current.

4.   Choose an empty space and draw the following shape (without dimensions):

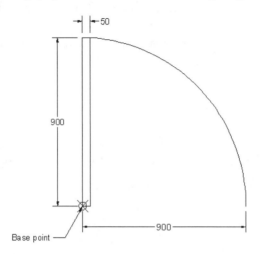

5.   Using the **Make Block** command, create a block using the following information:

    a.   Block name = Door

    b.   Specify the designated base point.

    c.   Delete the shape after the creation of the block.

    d.   Block unit = Millimeters

    e.   Scale uniformly = off, Allow exploding = on

    f.   Description = Door to be used inside the building. Refer to the door table.

    g.   Open in block editor = off

6.   Save the file and close it.

CREATING A BLOCK (IMPERIAL)

Workshop 3-B

1.   Start AutoCAD 2010.

2.   Open the file *Workshop_03.dwg*.

3.   Make layer 0 current.

4.   Choose an empty space and draw the following shape (without dimensions):

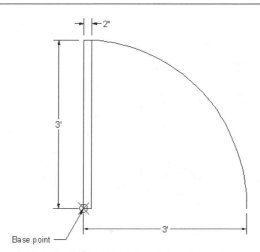

5. Using the **Make Block** command, create a block using the following information:
   a. Block name = Door
   b. Specify the designated base point.
   c. Delete the shape after the creation of the block.
   d. Block unit = Inches
   e. Scale uniformly = off, Allow exploding = on
   f. Description = Door to be used inside the building. Refer to the door table.
   g. Open in block editor = off
6. Save the file and close it.

6.3 INSERTING BLOCKS

- Once you create a block, you can use it in your drawing as many times as you wish.
- When inserting a block into your drawing, consider the following guidelines:
  - Set the desired layer to be current.
  - Prepare the drawing to accommodate the block (e.g., finish the door openings before inserting the door block).
- After you consider all of these guidelines, issue the command.

- Make sure you are in the **Home** tab on the **Ribbon**, and, using the **Block** panel, select the **Insert** button.

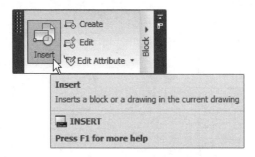

- The following dialog box will appear:

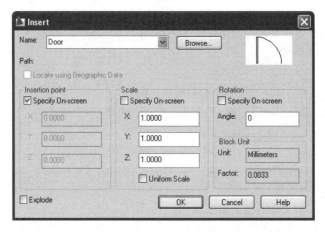

- Select the name of the desired block from the list.
- Specify the **Insertion point**, using one of two methods:
  - Click the **Specify On-screen** checkbox. By doing so, you will specify the insertion point using the mouse (this is easier than the next method).
  - Type the coordinates of the insertion point.
- Specify the **Scale** of the block by using one of the following methods:
  - Click the **Specify On-screen** checkbox. By doing so, you will specify the scale using the mouse.
  - Type the scale factor in all three directions of the insertion point. Because you can type in the scale factor, you can set the X-scale factor not equal to the Y-scale factor.
  - Another way to specify the scale is to click the **Uniform Scale** checkbox, which will allow you to input only one scale (the others will follow).

- Specify the **Rotation** of the block by using one of the following methods:
  - Click the **Specify On-screen** checkbox, which means you will specify the rotation angle using the mouse.
  - Type the rotation angle.
- The **Block unit** part will be read-only, thereby showing you the unit that you specified when you created this block. Also, it will show the **Factor** that is based on the **Block unit** and the **drawing unit** (which is defined in the **Drawing/Units** dialog box in the **Application Menu**). With this factor, AutoCAD will automatically scale the block to suit the current drawing.
- Click **OK** to end the command.

- Using the **Scale** of the block you can use negative values to insert mirror images of your block. See the following example:

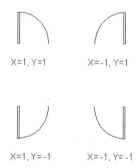

X=1, Y=1   X=-1, Y=1

X=1, Y=-1   X=-1, Y=-1

INSERTING BLOCKS (METRIC AND IMPERIAL)

Workshops 4-A and 4-B

1. Start AutoCAD 2010.
2. Open the file *Workshop_04.dwg*.
3. Make the layer **Doors** current.

4. Using the **Insert** command, insert the block **Door** in the proper places as shown:

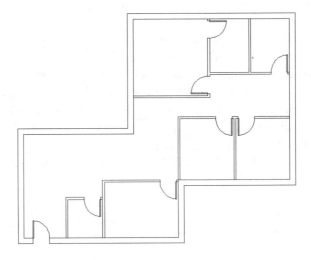

5. Save the file and close it.

6.4 EXPLODING BLOCKS

- When you insert incidences of blocks, keep them as blocks and do not try to change their nature.
- However, in some (rare) cases, you may want to explode the block (which is one object) to the objects forming it.
- To explode the block, you need to use the **Explode** command.
- Make sure you are in the **Home** tab on the **Ribbon**, and, using the **Modify** panel, select the **Explode** button.

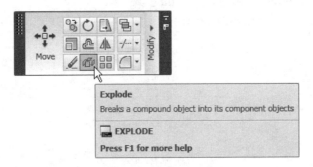

- AutoCAD will prompt you to:

```
Select objects:
```

- Once you are done, press [Enter] or right-click.
- Once you explode a block, it will go back to its original layer (the layer the block was created in).

NOTE
- Do not use this command unless you really need it.
- In older versions of AutoCAD, a block could not be defined as a cutting edge or a boundary edge in the **Trim** and **Extend** commands. Starting with AutoCAD 2005, you can select blocks as cutting edges and boundary edges. Therefore, there is no need to explode the block for this purpose.
- You can also use this command to explode polylines to lines and arcs.

6.5 USING DESIGN CENTER

- AutoCAD has a very helpful tool called **Design Center**, which allows the user to share blocks, layers, and other things between different files.
- In this chapter, we will concentrate on blocks.
- The file you want to take the blocks from could be anywhere:
  - It could be on your computer.
  - It could be on your colleague's computer, which is hooked up to the company's local area network.
  - It could be on a website.
- To start the **Design Center** command, make sure you are in the **View** tab on the **Ribbon**, and, using the **Palettes** panel, select the **Design Center** button.

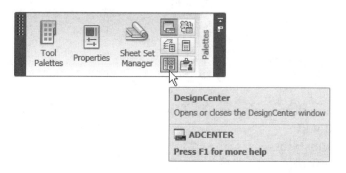

- The following will appear on the screen:

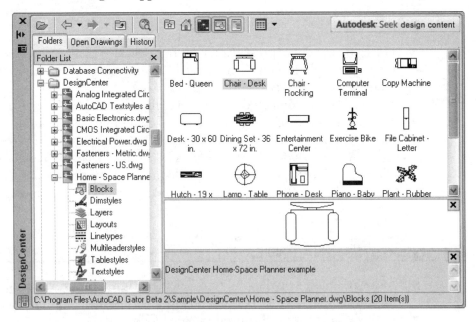

- As you can see, the **Design Center** palette is split into two parts:
  - On the left, you will see the hierarchy of your computer, including all your hard disks and network places (just like My Computer in Windows).
  - Select (by double-clicking) the desired hard disk, folder, and drawing, and you will see something like the following:

- As you can see, you can take from this drawing the following:
  - **Blocks**
  - **Dimstyles**
  - **Layers**
  - **Layouts**
  - **Linetypes**
  - **Multileaderstyles**

- **Tablestyles**
- **Textstyles**
- **Xrefs**
- Once you click the word **Blocks**, take a look at the right part of **Design Center**. You will see the blocks available in this drawing.
- There are several ways to move the blocks from this drawing to your drawing. They are:
  - Drag and drop (using the left button)
  - Drag and drop (using the right button)
  - Double-click
  - Right-click

Drag and Drop Using the Left Button

- Perform the following steps:
  - Make sure that you are in the right layer.
  - Make sure that you switched on the right **OSNAP** settings.
  - Click and hold the desired block.
  - Drag the block into your drawing; you will be holding it from the base point.
  - Once you catch the right **OSNAP**, release the mouse button.

Drag and Drop Using the Right Button

- Perform the following steps:
  - Make sure that you are in the right layer.
  - Make sure that you switched on the right **OSNAP** settings.
  - Right-click and hold the desired block.
  - Drag the block into your drawing.
  - Release the mouse button and the following shortcut menu will appear:

- It is the same as the **Insert** command discussed earlier.
- Follow the same steps as the **Insert** command.

Double-Click

- If you double-click any block in the **Design Center**, the **Insert** dialog box will appear and you can perform the same steps.

Right-Click

- Select the desired block and right-click. The following shortcut menu will appear:

- If you select **Insert Block**, the **Insert** dialog box will appear as discussed previously.
- You will notice two options, **Insert and Redefine** and **Redefine only**. We will be discussing redefining shortly.
- Select the **Block Editor** option if you want to open this block in the block editor in order to add dynamic features to it.
- If you select **Copy**, then you will copy the block to the clipboard of Windows, and you can use it in AutoCAD or in other software. To use it, select **Edit/Paste** or [Ctrl] + V.
- We will discuss the last option in the shortcut menu, the Tool Palette, shortly.

6.6 AUTOMATIC SCALING

- If you are using the **Design Center** to bring some blocks from other drawings and find that a block is either too large or too small, you will know that there is something wrong with the **Automatic Scaling** feature.
- To control the **Automatic Scaling** feature:
  - While you are creating the block make sure you are setting the right **Block unit**.
  - Before you bring the block from the **Design Center**, set the **Units to scale inserted contents** in the **Drawing/Units** option of the **Application Menu**.

Block Unit

- When you are creating a block, the following dialog box will appear:

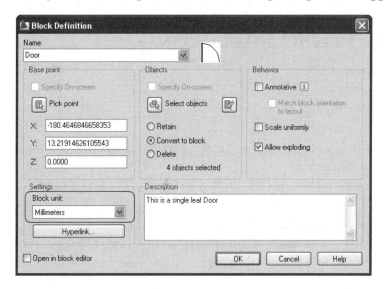

- Under the area labeled **Block unit**, select the desired unit.

Units to Scale Inserted Contents

- Before using any block, select **Drawing/Units** from the **Application Menu** and the following dialog box will appear:

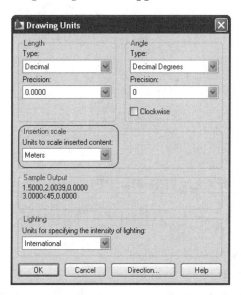

- Under the area labeled **Units to scale inserted contents**, set the desired scale used in your drawing.
- Using the two scales, AutoCAD will calculate the proper scale for the block.

USING THE DESIGN CENTER (METRIC)

Workshop 5-A

1. Start AutoCAD 2010.
2. Open the file *Workshop_05.dwg*.
3. Make the **Furniture** layer current.
4. Select **Format/Units** and make sure that **Units to scale inserted content** is **millimeters**.
5. Open the **Design Center**. From the left part of the **Design Center** palette double-click the drive containing the AutoCAD 2010 folder.
6. Select **AutoCAD 2010/Sample/Design Center**.
7. Using *Home Space Planner.dwg*, *House Designer.dwg*, and *Kitchens.dwg* while **OSNAP** is off, drag and drop the following blocks as shown:

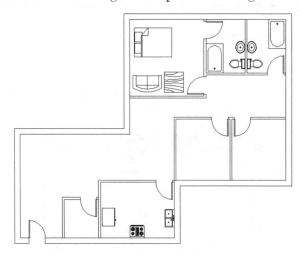

8. Save the file and close it.

USING THE DESIGN CENTER (IMPERIAL)

Workshop 5-B

1. Start AutoCAD 2010.
2. Open the file *Workshop_05.dwg*.
3. Make the **Furniture** layer current.
4. Select **Format/Units** and make sure that **Units to scale inserted content** is in **inches**.

5. Open the **Design Center**. From the left part of the **Design Center** palette double-click the drive containing the AutoCAD 2010 folder.

6. Select **AutoCAD 2010/Sample/Design Center**.

7. Using *Home Space Planner.dwg*, *House Designer.dwg*, and *Kitchens.dwg* while **OSNAP** is off, drag and drop the following blocks as shown:

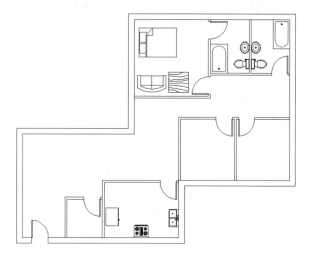

8. Save the file and close it.

6.7 WHAT IS A TOOL PALETTE?

- The **Design Center** gives us the ability to share data from other files. However, you need to make sure you are at the right layer and specify the rotation angle, scale factor, etc. Also, you need to search for the desired content each and every time.
- **Tool Palette** will solve all of these problems.
- **Tool Palette** will keep blocks, hatch, and other items available for you regardless of which drawing you are using. You can keep virtually anything inside a Tool Palette.
- **Tool Palette** works with the same drag-and-drop method we used with the **Design Center**, but in **Tool Palette** the method will be done in two ways: from **Tool Palette** and to **Tool Palette**.
- **Tool Palette** is unique per computer in the sense that it is not limited to one particular drawing. Therefore, if you create/customize a Tool Palette, it will be available for all your drawings.

- To start the **Tool Palette** command, make sure you are in the **View** tab on the **Ribbon**, and, using the **Palettes** panel, select the **Tool Palettes** button:

- The following will appear on the screen:

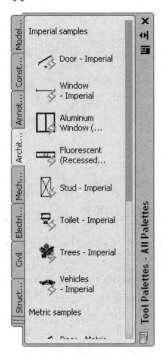

- You will see several premade Tool Palettes by Autodesk® for your immediate use.
- Depending on the source, you can create your own Tool Palette using different methods.
- You can copy, cut, and paste tools inside each Tool Palette.
- You can customize the tools inside each Tool Palette.

6.8 CREATING A TOOL PALETTE

Creating a Tool Palette from Scratch

- Right-click over the name of any existing Tool Palette and the following shortcut menu will appear:

- Select the **New Palette** option and a new Tool Palette will be added. Type in the name of the new Tool Palette.

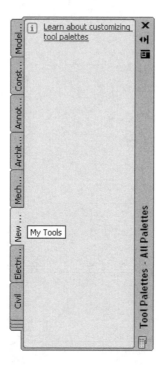

- A new empty Tool Palette will be added.
- To fill this Tool Palette, use the drag-and-drop method either from the **Graphical Area** or from the **Design Center**.

▪ By default, the local blocks of the current drawing are not automatically available in your Tool Palettes.

Example

▪ Assume we have the following drawing in front of us. This drawing contains polylines, hatch, and a linear dimension:

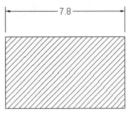

▪ Without issuing any commands, click on the polyline, then hold it (avoiding the blue rectangles) and drag it into the empty Tool Palette. Do the same thing for the hatch and the linear dimension. Your Tool Palette will look like the following:

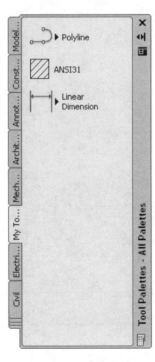

Creating a Tool Palette Using the **Design Center**

- You can copy all of the blocks in one drawing using the **Design Center** and create a Tool Palette from them, retaining the name of the drawing.
- To do that, follow these steps:
  - Start **Design Center**.
  - Go to the desired folder, then to the desired file.
  - Right-click on the **Blocks** icon and the following shortcut menu will appear:

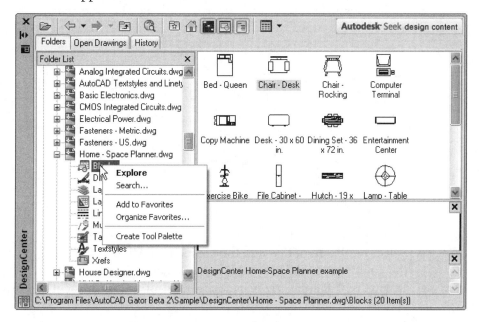

- Select the **Create Tool Palette** option and a new Tool Palette will be added with the name of the file you chose. It will include all of the blocks.
- You can also drag and drop any block from the **Design Center** to any desired Tool Palette.

6.9 CUSTOMIZING A TOOL PALETTE

- Blocks and hatch in a Tool Palette can be copied and then pasted in the same Tool Palette or in any other Tool Palette.
- The purpose of this option is to assign different properties to each tool.

- For example, there is a block called **chair** and you want to make three copies of it. Each copy would hold a different rotation angle. The same thing applies to hatch patterns, as each copy can have a different scale factor.
- Also, you can specify that a certain block (or hatch) go to a certain layer regardless of the current layer.

How to Copy and Paste a Tool

- Follow these steps:
  - Right-click on the desired tool and the following shortcut menu will appear:

  - Select the **Copy** option.
  - Select the **Paste** option and the copied tool will reside at the bottom of the Tool Palette, and will hold the same name.
  - In any Tool Palette, right-click and the following shortcut menu will appear:

How to Customize a Tool

- ▪ Follow these steps:
  - • Right-click on the copied tool and the following shortcut menu will appear:

  - • Select the **Properties** option and the following dialog box will appear:

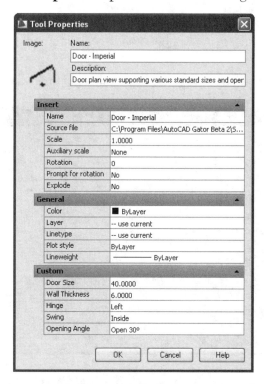

- ▪ You can change the name and description of the tool.
- ▪ There are two types of properties:
  - • **Insert** properties, where a block's properties are different from a hatch's properties.

- **General** properties, such as color, layer, linetype, plot style, and lineweight.

- By default, the **General** properties are all **use current**, which means use the current settings.

- All **Insert** properties and **General** properties are changeable.

- In the **Tool Properties** dialog box, if the image of the block is not clear, you can change it. To do so, perform the following steps:

    - Go to the image, right-click, and a shortcut menu will appear:

    - Select **Specify image** and the following dialog box will appear:

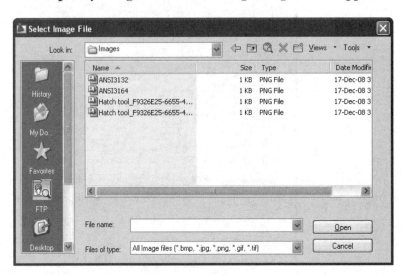

    - Select the desired folder and the desired file and click **Open**. Now the new image will appear.

USING AND CUSTOMIZING TOOL PALETTES (METRIC AND IMPERIAL)

 Workshops 6-A and 6-B

1. Start AutoCAD 2010.

2. Start a new file.

3. Make layer 0 current.

4. Open the **Design Center**. From the left part of the **Design Center** palette double-click the drive containing the AutoCAD 2010 folder.

5. Select **AutoCAD 2010/Sample/Design Center**.

6. Select the file *Home Space Planner.dwg*.

7. Right-click the **Blocks** icon and select **Create Tool Palette**. A new Tool Palette with the name **Home Space Planner** will be added.

8. Select the file *House Designer.dwg*.

9. Show the blocks for this file.

10. Locate **Bath Tub –26 × 60 in** block and drag and drop it in your newly created Tool Palette.

11. Do the same with the **Sink Oval Top** block.

12. Right-click on the name of the Tool Palette and select **Rename**, and change the name to **My Tools**.

13. In the **My Tools** Tool Palette, right-click on the tool named **Chair–Rocking**, and select **Properties**. In the dialog box, change the **Layer** from **use current** to **Furniture**.

14. Right-click on the same tool again and select **Copy**. Select an empty space and **Paste** it three times.

15. Using the same method in Step 13, change the rotation angle of these blocks to be 90, –90, 180.

16. Now you have a tool palette that you can use in all your drawings on this computer.

6.10 EDITING BLOCKS

- Assume that after you created a block and have inserted it into your drawing several times, you discover that there is something wrong with it.

- To solve your problem, you need to redefine the original block using **Block Editor**.

- In the block editor, you can create a **Dynamic Block** (an advanced feature in AutoCAD, but for now we will use it only to edit blocks).

- To start the **Block Editor** command, make sure you are in the **Home** tab on the **Ribbon**, and, using the **Block** panel, select the **Edit** button.

- AutoCAD will show the following dialog box:

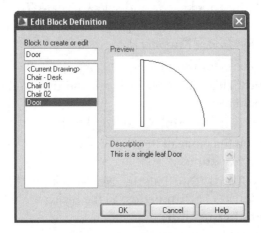

- Select the name of the block to be edited and click **OK**.
- The **Block Editor** will open. A new tab with many new panels will be added titled **Block Editor**.
- You should not be intimidated by these changes, simply ignore them, and make all the changes you need to your block (adding, modifying, and erasing).
- Once you are done, click the **Close Block Editor** button on the right and the following message will appear:

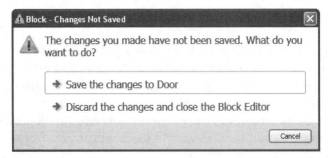

- You have two choices, either to save the changes to the block, or simply to discard these changes.

- If you double-click on a block, it will start the same command.

EDITING BLOCKS (METRIC)

Workshop 7-A
1. Start AutoCAD 2010.
2. Open the file *Workshop_07.dwg*.
3. Start the **Edit** command in the **Block** panel.
4. Select one of the doors you inserted. Once the dialog box appears, click **OK**.
5. Select the arc representing the swing of the door. Right-click and select **Properties**.
6. Change its layer to **Door_Swing**.
7. Change the Linetype scale = 200.
8. Close the **Properties** palette.
9. Click **Save changes**.
10. You will see now that all the door swings change to dashed linetype.
11. Save the file and close it.

EDITING BLOCKS (IMPERIAL)

Workshop 7-B
1. Start AutoCAD 2010.
2. Open the file *Workshop_07.dwg*.
3. Start the **Edit** command in the **Block** panel.
4. Select one of the doors you inserted. Once the dialog box appears, click **OK**.
5. Select the arc representing the swing of the door. Right-click and select **Properties**.
6. Change its layer to be **Door_Swing**.
7. Change the Linetype scale = 10.
8. Close the **Properties** palette.
9. Click **Save changes**.
10. You will see now that all the door swings change to dashed linetype.
11. Save the file and close it.

CHAPTER REVIEW

1. You should draw your original shape, which will be a block, in layer 0.
   a. True
   b. False
2. The **Automatic Scaling** feature in AutoCAD:
   a. Will change the scale of the block to fit in the current drawing.
   b. Will require two scales to convert the block.
   c. Will work for both blocks and hatch.
   d. None of the above.
3. Which of the following statements is true about Tool Palettes?
   a. They can be created from blocks coming from the **Design Center**.
   b. You can drag and drop to and from a Tool Palette.
   c. You can customize the block inside a Tool Palette.
   d. All of the above.
4. Which of the following commands cannot be used for blocks?
   a. **Explode**
   b. **Insert**
   c. **Makelocalblock**
   d. **Block Editor**
5. In order to make the **Design Center** and **Tool Palettes** occupy less space in the **Graphical Area**, use _____.

CHAPTER REVIEW ANSWERS

1. a
2. a
3. d
4. c
5. Auto-hide

Chapter **7** **HATCHING**

In This Chapter

7.1 HATCHING IN AUTOCAD®

- In order to hatch in AutoCAD® you need to draw objects forming a closed area. Beginning with AutoCAD 2005, it became acceptable to hatch an area with a small opening.
- AutoCAD comes with several generic predefined hatch patterns saved in one of two files called *acad.pat* and *acadiso.pat*. You can also buy other hatch patterns from third parties, which can be found on the Internet.
- A hatch, like any other object, should be placed in a separate layer.
- There are two methods to hatch in AutoCAD: the old method (**Hatch** command) and the new method (**Tool Palette**).

7.2 SELECTING THE HATCH PATTERN

- This is the old method of hatching in AutoCAD.
- To start the **Hatch** command, make sure you are in the **Home** tab on the **Ribbon**, and, using the **Draw** panel, select the **Hatch** button.

- The following dialog box will appear:

- Under the **Hatch** tab, select the **Type** pop-up list and you will see the following choices:

User Defined

- ■ The simplest hatch pattern has parallel lines. Once this option is selected, the following parameters will be valid:
  - • **Swatch**: displays a preview of the hatch.
  - • **Angle**: defines the angle of the parallel lines.
  - • **Spacing**: defines the distance between two parallel lines.
  - • **Double**: means "in both ways."
- ■ The following is a **User defined** hatch, using **Angle** = 45 and **Double** hatch:

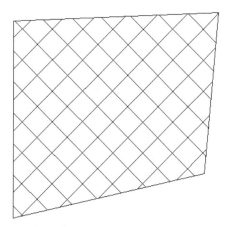

Predefined

- ■ There are a handful of hatch patterns available for use. You will see **ANSI** hatches, **ISO** hatches, and commonly used hatches. The following are the parameters to be set:
  - • **Pattern**: whether you select the desired pattern using the pop-up list, select the small button with the three dots, or click **Swatch**, the following dialog box will appear showing the **ANSI** hatches:

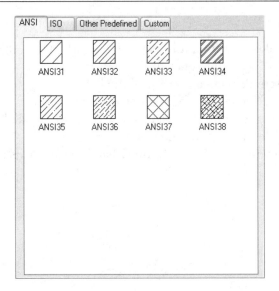

- Click the **ISO** tab and you will see the following:

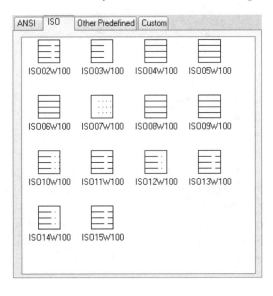

- Click the **Other Predefined** tab and you will see the following:

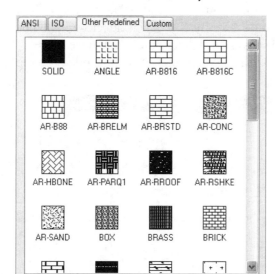

- When you are done selecting the hatch pattern, click **OK**.
- Set the **Angle**.
- Set the **Scale** of the hatch pattern.
- If you select one of the **ISO** hatches, set the **ISO pen width**.

Custom

- If you customized a hatch pattern or bought some from a third party, they should be used using the **Custom** tab.

7.3 SELECTING THE AREA TO BE HATCHED

- After you pick your hatch pattern and set the relative parameters, you need to select the desired area to be hatched.
- You can select more than one area with the same command, but the hatch will be considered either as one object or as separate objects.
- There are two ways to select the objects forming the area:
  - **Add Pick points**
  - **Add Select objects**

Add Pick Points

- This method is very simple. Click inside the desired area and AutoCAD will recognize the area automatically.

- This method will also detect any objects (called islands) within the outer area, and deselect them automatically. The islands will not be hatched.
- Islands can be any object type: circle, closed polyline, text, etc.

NOTE ▶
- We will discuss island detection in detail, shortly.
- Click the **Add: Pick points** button located at the top right-hand part of the dialog box.

- The dialog box will disappear temporarily and the following prompt will appear:

```
Pick internal point or [Select objects/remove
Boundaries]:
```

- Click inside the desired area(s). When you are done, press [Enter] or right-click and then select the **Enter** option. The dialog box will reappear.

Add Select Objects

- This is the same method used to select any object, as previously discussed.
- Click the **Add: Select objects** button located at the top right-hand part of the dialog box.

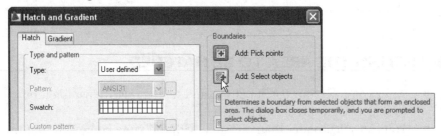

- The dialog box will disappear temporarily and the following prompt will appear:

```
Select objects or [pick internal point/remove
Boundaries]:
```

- Select the desired objects that form a closed area. When you are done, press [Enter] or right-click and then select the **Enter** option. The dialog box will reappear.

- After you have made your selection, you will be able to do two things:
  - **Remove boundaries**: you will most likely need this button when using **Add: Pick points**. **Add: Pick points** will select all the inner objects and text as islands and this button will allow you to remove some of the selected objects as islands.
  - **View Selections**: use this button to view the selection set to make sure that it is the right one.

7.4 PREVIEWING THE HATCH

- The data input is now complete, you have selected the hatch pattern along with its parameters, and you have selected the area to be hatched. The next step is to preview the hatch before you make the final decision to accept the outcome.
- Click the **Preview** button located at the lower left-hand corner of the dialog box:

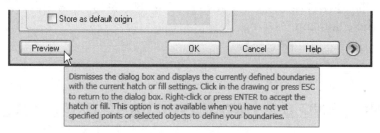

- The dialog box will disappear temporarily.
- You will see the results of your settings (i.e., hatch pattern, angle, scale, islands, etc.). Accordingly, AutoCAD will prompt you to:

```
Pick or press Esc to return to dialog or <Right-
click to accept hatch>:
```

- If you like what you see, right-click or press [Enter], otherwise, press [Esc].

- If you pressed [Esc], the dialog box will reappear and you can change any of the parameters, preview again, and so on.

HATCHING USING THE HATCH COMMAND (METRIC)

Workshop 8-A
1. Start AutoCAD 2010.
2. Open the file *Workshop_08.dwg*.
3. Make the **Hatch** layer current.
4. Start the **Hatch** command and select the **Type** as **Predefined**.
5. Click on **Swatch** and select the **Other Predefined** tab. Select the **AR-CONC** pattern.
6. Set the **Scale** = 100.
7. Click on the **Add: Pick points** button, and click inside the area representing the outer wall. Press [Enter].
8. Click **Preview** to see the results of the hatching, then press [Enter] to end the command.
9. Start the **Hatch** command again and select the **Type** as **Predefined**.
10. Click on **Swatch** and select the **ANSI** tab. Select the **ANSI32** pattern.
11. Set the **Scale** = 500.
12. Click on the **Add: Pick points** button, and click inside the area representing the inner walls. Press [Enter].
13. Click **Preview** to see the results of the hatching, then press [Enter] to end the command.
14. Save the file and close it.

HATCHING USING THE HATCH COMMAND (IMPERIAL)

Workshop 8-B
1. Start AutoCAD 2010.
2. Open the file *Workshop_08.dwg*.
3. Make the **Hatch** layer current.
4. Start the **Hatch** command and select the **Type** as **Predefined**.
5. Click on **Swatch** and select the **Other Predefined** tab. Select the **AR-CONC** pattern.
6. Set the **Scale** = 5.

7. Click on the **Add: Pick points** button and click inside the area representing the outer wall. Press [Enter].

8. Click **Preview** to see the results of the hatching, then press [Enter] to end the command.

9. Start the **Hatch** command again and select the **Type** as **Predefined**.

10. Click on **Swatch** and select the **ANSI** tab. Select the **ANSI32** pattern.

11. Set the **Scale** = 20.

12. Click on the **Add: Pick points** button and click inside the area representing the inner walls. Press [Enter].

13. Click **Preview** to see the results of the hatching, then press [Enter] to end the command.

14. Save the file and close it.

7.5 HATCHING OPTIONS

- While you are hatching, there are some options in the **Hatch** command that you should know in order to have full control over the hatching process.

- At the right side of the dialog box, there is a part labeled **Options**:

Annotative

- This is an advanced feature related to printing.

Associative

- Associative means that there is a relationship between the hatch and the boundary. Whenever the boundary changes, the hatch changes automatically. It is recommended to keep this option selected.

Example

- Assume you have the following shape, which you want to hatch:

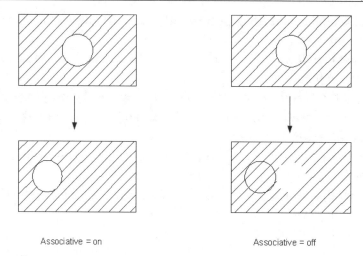

Associative = on   Associative = off

Create Separate Hatches

- By default, when you hatch several areas using the same command, all of the hatches will be considered one object. They will be moved together and erased together.
- Using the **Create separate hatches** option, you can hatch several areas using the same command and each hatch will be considered a separate object. To do so, click the **Create separate hatches** checkbox.

Draw Order

- If hatched areas are intersecting with other hatched areas (specifically hatched with **Solid** hatching), you need to set the **Draw** order while you are inserting the hatch to ensure the right appearance of each area.
- The four options are:
  - **Send to back** (see the following)
  - **Bring to front** (see the following)

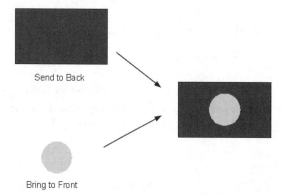

Send to Back

Bring to Front

- **Send behind boundary** (see the following)
- **Bring in front of boundary** (see the following)

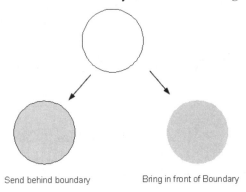

Send behind boundary   Bring in front of Boundary

Inherit Properties

- Below the **Options** part is the **Inherit Properties** button:

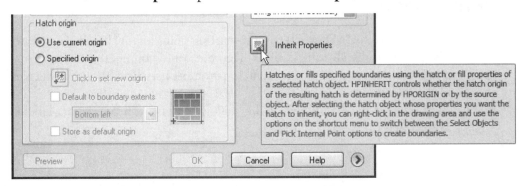

- The purpose of this button is to help users quickly hatch a new area with the same exact features of an existing hatch.
- Click the **Inherit Properties** button and the dialog box will disappear temporarily. The following prompt will appear:

```
Select hatch object:
```

- The mouse will change to a paintbrush:

- Click the source hatch pattern and the following steps will occur.
  - A new prompt will appear:

```
Inherited Properties: Name <SOLID>, Scale <1.0000>,
Angle <0>
Pick internal point or [Select objects/remove
Boundaries]:
```

- Meanwhile, the cursor will change to a bigger paintbrush, with small crosshairs, so you can click inside the new areas you want to hatch:

- Click inside the desired area(s). When you are done, press [Enter] or right-click and select the **Enter** option. The dialog box will reappear. Click **OK** to finish the command.

7.6 HATCH ORIGIN

- By default, AutoCAD uses 0,0 as the starting point for any hatch. Therefore, if you want to hatch using a brick-like hatch, and you need it to start from a point in the area you want to hatch, you must use the settings in this part of the dialog box.
- At the lower left-hand side of the dialog box you will see a part labeled **Hatch origin**:

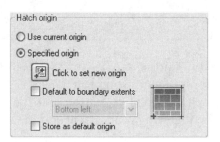

- Click the **Specified origin** radio button.
- In order to specify a new origin, you have two options:
  - Use the **Click to set new origin** button and select any point you desire.
  - Click the **Default to boundary extents** checkbox and select one of the options available: Bottom left, Bottom right, Top left, Top right, or Center. You can also store this choice as the default origin.

- See the following example:

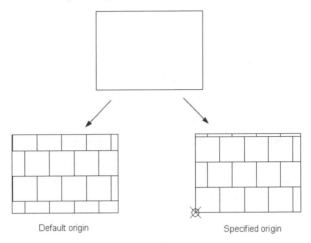

Default origin   Specified origin

ASSOCIATIVE HATCHING AND HATCH ORIGIN (METRIC)

Workshop 9-A

1. Start AutoCAD 2010.
2. Open the file *Workshop_09.dwg*.
3. Make the **Hatch** layer current.
4. Zoom to the kitchen at the lower right of the plan.
5. Start the **Hatch** command and select the **Type** as **Predefined**.
6. Click on **Swatch** and select the **Other Predefined** tab. Select the **ANGLE** pattern.
7. Set the **Scale** = 1000. Set the **Hatch origin** = Use current origin. Also, make sure that **Associative** is on.
8. Click on the **Add: Pick points** button and click inside the area representing the bathroom. Press [Enter].
9. Click **Preview** to see the results of the hatching. Press [Esc] and you will see the dialog box again. Select **Specified origin** and specify the lower left corner of the kitchen to be the new origin. Click **Preview** again. Do you see a change? Press [Enter] to finish the command.
10. Move the oven to the right. What is happening to the hatch? Does it react correctly or not?
11. Save the file and close it.

ASSOCIATIVE HATCHING AND HATCH ORIGIN (IMPERIAL)

 Workshop 9-B

1. Start AutoCAD 2010.
2. Open the file *Workshop_09.dwg*.
3. Make the **Hatch** layer current.
4. Zoom to the kitchen at the lower right of the plan.
5. Start the **Hatch** command and select the **Type** as **Predefined**.
6. Click on **Swatch** and select the **Other Predefined** tab. Select the **ANGLE** pattern.
7. Set the **Scale** = 50. Set the **Hatch origin** = Use current origin. Also, make sure that **Associative** is on.
8. Click on the **Add: Pick points** button and click inside the area representing the bathroom. Press [Enter].
9. Click **Preview** to see the results of the hatching. Press [Esc] and you will see the dialog box again. Select **Specified origin** and specify the lower left-hand corner of the kitchen to be the new origin. Click **Preview** again. Do you see a change? Press [Enter] to finish the command.
10. Move the oven to the right. What is happening to the hatch? Does it react correctly or not?
11. Save the file and close it.

7.7 ADVANCED FEATURES

- At the lower right-hand corner of the dialog box, you will see a small button with an arrow pointing to the right. Click this button to see more advanced options for hatching:

Islands

- The first is the **Islands** option:

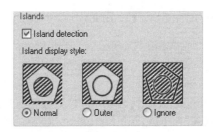

- Islands in AutoCAD are the objects inside the outer boundary of an area to be hatched.
  - Click **Island detection** off if you do not want AutoCAD to recognize the inner objects.
  - Click **Island detection** on if you want AutoCAD to select the inner objects as boundaries and do not want to hatch them.
- Select one of three styles:
  - **Normal**: If three or more objects are nested inside each other, AutoCAD will hatch the outer, leave the second, hatch the third, etc.
  - **Outer**: If three or more objects are nested inside each other, AutoCAD will only hatch the outer, leaving the inner objects intact.
  - **Ignore**: If three or more objects are nested inside each other, AutoCAD will ignore all the inner objects and only hatch the outer area.

Boundary Retention

- By default, AutoCAD creates a polyline around the detected area. Once the **Hatch** command is finished, AutoCAD will delete this polyline.
  - The **Boundary retention** option allows you to keep this temporary polyline.

  - Click the **Retain boundaries** checkbox and specify the **Object type** as either **Polyline** or **Region**.

Boundary Set

- When using the **Add: Pick points** option to define the boundary to be hatched, AutoCAD will analyze all of the objects in the **Current viewport** by default.
- This could take a long time depending on the complexity of the drawing. To minimize the time, you can provide a selection set for AutoCAD to analyze the boundary.

- The **Boundary** set part of the dialog box looks like this:

- By default, the selected option is **Current viewport**.
- Click the **New** button and the dialog box will disappear temporarily. The following prompt will appear:

```
Select objects:
```

- Select the desired objects and press [Enter] or right-click. The dialog box will appear again, but this time the selected option will be **Existing set**, as follows:

- Now, when you ask AutoCAD to select a boundary by clicking inside it, AutoCAD will not analyze all of the objects in the current viewport, but instead will only analyze the objects in the set you have selected.

Gap Tolerance

- AutoCAD accepts an area with a small gap to hatch. The size is defined by the user.
- You can set the maximum gap that AutoCAD may ignore:

Inherit Options

- This section deals with two things previously discussed: **Inherit Properties** and **Hatch origin**.
- When you select **Inherit Properties** from an existing hatch, you have two options to choose from:
  - **Use current origin**
  - **Use source hatch origin**

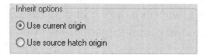

7.8 HATCHING USING TOOL PALETTES

- Previously, we introduced the concept of **Tool Palettes**, which includes both blocks and hatches.
- The main feature of **Tool Palettes** is the drag-and-drop feature. We will utilize this feature to speed up the process of hatching.
- Perform the following steps:
  - Create a new Tool Palette (for example, call it "My Hatches").
  - Use the **Hatch** command to add hatches to your different drawings.
  - While you are hatching, you are changing the hatch settings.
  - Each time you would like this hatch with all of its settings to be used in other drawings, simply drag and drop it into your newly created Tool Palette.
  - You can make several copies of your hatch. Then, you can customize the different settings of each hatch. Right-click on any hatch in your Tool Palette and select **Properties**. The following dialog box will appear:

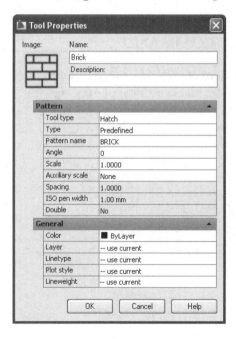

- After several drawings, you will have a large library of hatches that you can use in your drawings.
- Now, use the drag-and-drop feature to move hatches from your Tool Palettes to your drawing.
- By default, there will be a Tool Palette called **Hatches and Fills** that you can use if you do not wish to create your own.

HATCHING AND TOOL PALETTE (METRIC AND IMPERIAL)

Workshop 10-A and 10-B

1. Start AutoCAD 2010.
2. Open the file *Workshop_10.dwg*.
3. Start **Tool Palettes**. Create a new Tool Palette and name it **My Hatches**.
4. Drag and drop the three hatches we used in our file, which are: **AR-CONC**, **ANSI32**, and **ANGLE**.
5. In the new Tool Palette, select any of the three hatches and right-click. Select **Properties** and make sure that the current layer is always **Hatch** and not **use current**.
6. Next time you use the hatch from the Tool Palette, you will not worry about which layer the hatch will reside in.
7. Save the file and close it.

7.9 THE GRADIENT COMMAND

-   Use the **Gradient** command if you to want to shade a 2D area with one color along with white, black, a shade of gray, or with two colors.
-   The **Gradient** command uses the same method as the **Hatch** command, so there is no need to describe the steps again.
-   To start the **Gradient** command, make sure you are in the **Home** tab on the **Ribbon**, and, expanding the **Draw** panel, select the **Gradient** button.

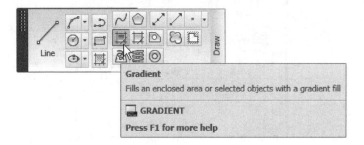

-   The following dialog box will appear:

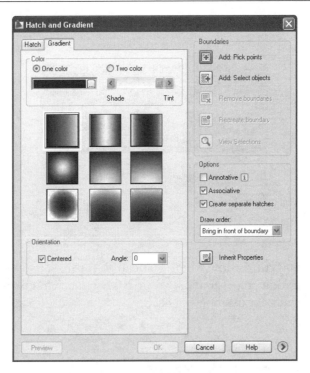

- Begin by specifying whether you want to use one color along with white, or two colors:

- If you select **One color**, then you will need to do the following:
  - Click the small button (with the three dots in it) to select the desired color.
  - Move the slider from **Tint** (total white) to **Shade** (total black), or any color in between the two.
- If you select **Two color**, the following will appear:

Selecting a Color

- There are three sets of colors you can select from: **Index Color**, **True Color**, and **Color Books**.

- 255 colors, called **Index Color**.

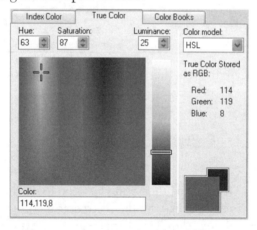

- 24-bit **True Color**, where you can select from two models: **HSL** (Hue, Saturation, and Luminance) or **RGB** (Red, Green, and Blue). See the following for examples of each.

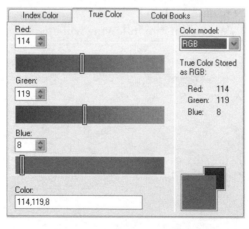

- You can also select a color from one of 11 **Color Books** available:

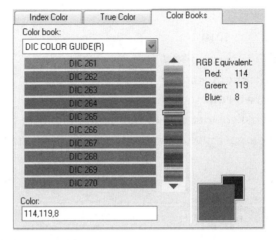

- Now, select one of the nine gradient patterns:

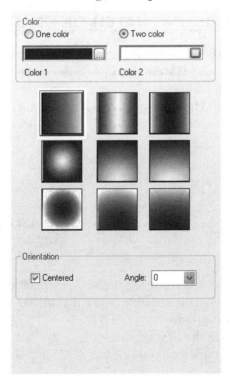

- Select whether your pattern is symmetrical (**Centered**) or not, and then select the angle of the pattern.
- The rest of the steps are identical to the **Hatch** command.

USING THE GRADIENT COMMAND

 Exercise 33
1. Start AutoCAD 2010.
2. Open the file *Exercise_33.dwg*.
3. Start the **Gradient** command.
4. Select the **Two color** option.
5. Select the first color to be 142 and the second to be 61.
6. Choose the upper-middle method to define how the two colors should be mixed.
7. Select the inner area.
8. Preview the gradient.
9. Save the file and close it.

7.10 EDITING AN EXISTING HATCH OR GRADIENT

- Use the **Edit Hatch** command if you want to edit an existing hatch (whether you are using the **Hatch** command, the drag-and-drop method, or the **Gradient** command).
- To start the **Edit Hatch** command, make sure you are in the **Home** tab on the **Ribbon**, and, expanding the **Modify** panel, select the **Edit Hatch** button.

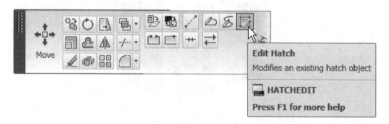

- There are other ways to reach the same command:
  - Right-click on the desired hatch. From the shortcut menu select the **Hatch Edit** option.
  - Double-click the desired hatch.
- Regardless of the method used, AutoCAD will show the following prompt:

```
Select hatch object:
```

- Select the desired hatch and the **Hatch** dialog box will appear. Change the settings as you wish and click **OK**.

- Other ways to edit a hatch or gradient include:
  - **Quick Properties**
  - **Properties**
  - Double-clicking

Quick Properties

- Whenever you select a hatch, the **Quick Properties** window will appear. You can make the most important edits you need here:

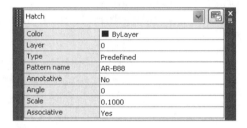

Properties

- Select the hatch, right-click, and select **Properties** from the shortcut menu. The following **Properties** palette will appear:

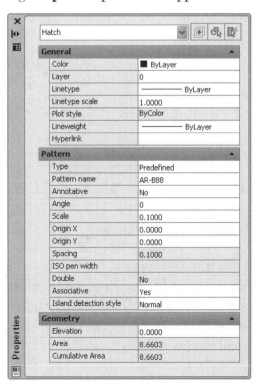

- In the **Properties** palette you can edit all of the data related to the hatch selected (some of the settings will be applicable to user-defined hatch patterns such as **Spacing** and **Double**).

Recreate Boundary

- If you hatched an area, and for some reason the boundary was lost but the hatch was kept, you can use this option to recreate the boundary of an existing hatch.
- Double-click the hatch without the boundary. The **Hatch** dialog box will appear. Perform the following steps:
    - Click the **Recreate boundary** button. The dialog will disappear temporarily.

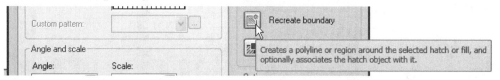

- The following prompt will appear:

```
Enter type of boundary object [Region/Polyline]
<Polyline>:
```

- Type **P** for polyline or **R** for region, and the following prompt will appear:

```
Associate hatch with new boundary? [Yes/No] <Y>:
```

- Type **Y** for yes or **N** for no.
- The dialog box will appear again. Click **OK** to finish the command.

EDIT HATCHING (METRIC)

Workshop 11-A

1. Start AutoCAD 2010.
2. Open the file *Workshop_11.dwg*.
3. Select the **AR-CONC** hatch, right-click, and then select **Hatch Edit**. The **Hatch Edit** dialog box will appear. Set the **Scale** = 75.
4. Click **Preview** and press [Enter] to accept the changes you made.
5. Double-click the **ANGLE** hatch and set the **Angle** = 45.
6. Click **Preview** and press [Enter] to accept the changes you made.
7. Save the file and close it.

EDIT HATCHING (IMPERIAL)

Workshop 11-B

1. Start AutoCAD 2010.
2. Open the file *Workshop_11.dwg*.
3. Select the **AR-CONC** hatch, right-click, and then select **Hatch Edit**. The **Hatch Edit** dialog box will appear. Set the **Scale** = 2.5.
4. Click **Preview** and press [Enter] to accept the changes you made.
5. Double-click the **ANGLE** hatch and set the **Angle** = 45.
6. Click **Preview** and press [Enter] to accept the changes you made.
7. Save the file and close it.

CHAPTER REVIEW

1. The origin of a hatch area is defined by AutoCAD and you cannot change it.
   a. True
   b. False
2. You can create a boundary for an existing hatch using the_____
   ____ button.
3. AutoCAD now supports 24-bit **True Color**.
   a. True
   b. False
4. Which of these statements is NOT true about hatching in AutoCAD?
   a. You can set the **Draw** order of the hatch.
   b. You can use the conventional method and the drag-and-drop method.
   c. The desired area must be closed in order to hatch it.
   d. You can use hatch or gradient colors.
5. Which of the following tasks cannot be done using the **Hatch** command?
   a. Separate hatches using the same command.
   b. Hatching areas with gap.
   c. Set the scale of the hatch pattern.
   d. Hatch with a three-color gradient.
6. If you want the hatch to react to any change in the boundary, click the _____ checkbox in the **Hatch** dialog box.

CHAPTER REVIEW ANSWERS

1. b
2. Recreate boundary
3. a
4. c
5. d
6. Associative

Chapter **8** **TEXT AND TABLES**

In This Chapter

◊ Introduction
◊ **Text Style**
◊ **Single Line Text**
◊ **Multiline Text**
◊ An Introduction to Editing Text
◊ Editing Text Using **Quick Properties** and **Properties**
◊ Text and Grips
◊ **Check Spelling** and **Find and Replace**
◊ **Table Style**
◊ The **Table** Command

8.1 INTRODUCTION

- In order to input text in AutoCAD® you first need to create your own text style.
- In **Text Style**, you will specify the characteristics of all the text you input into your drawing file.
- You should have several text styles in your drawing in order to cover all of the requirements (large fonts for titles, small fonts for remarks, special text style for dimensions, etc.).
- Text styles can be shared between files using **Design Center**.
- After you create your text style, you can use several commands to input text into your drawing:
  - **Single line text** (old method)
  - **Multiline text** (new method)
- After you finish writing, you can edit and check the spelling of the text.
- In order to create tables with text, you have to create a **Table Style**.

- You can insert tables and write text inside them.
- Table styles can be shared between files using **Design Center**.

8.2 TEXT STYLE

- The first step in writing text in AutoCAD is to create a text style.
- **Text Style** is where you define the characteristics of your text.
- To start the **Text Style** command, make sure you are in the **Home** tab on the **Ribbon**, and, expanding the **Annotation** panel, select the **Text Style** button:

- The following dialog box will appear:

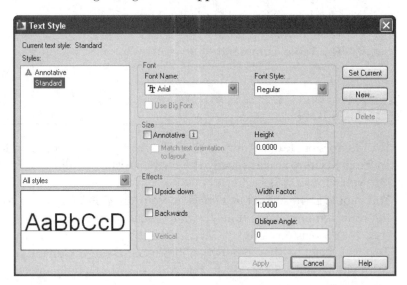

- As you can see, AutoCAD comes with a default text style called **Standard**.
- This style contains the default settings of the text style.
- This style is very simple and you should consider creating your own.
- To create a new text style, click the **New** button and the following dialog box will appear:

- Type in the name of the new text style using the same naming convention you used with the layers.
- When done, click **OK**.

Font Name

- The first thing to do is to select the desired font.
- There are two types of fonts you can use in AutoCAD:
  - **Shape Files** (**.shx*), the old type of fonts.
  - **True Type** fonts (**.ttf*), the new type of fonts.
- The following illustration shows the difference between the two types:

True Type Font

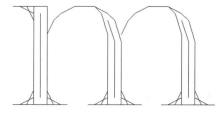

Shape File

Font Style

- If you select a **True Type** font, you will be able to select the **Font Style**. You can choose from the following:
  - Regular
  - Bold
  - Bold Italic
  - Italic
- See the following illustration:

Regular   Bold   Bold/Italic   Italic

Annotative

- This is an advanced feature; we will leave it off for this example.

Height

- Specify the **height** of the text. See the following illustration:

- As you can see, the height mentioned in the dialog box is for the capital letters.
- There are two methods for specifying the height of text:
  - Leave the value equal to 0 (zero), which means you have to specify the height each and every time you use this style.
  - Specify a height value that will always be used once you have created this style.

Effects

- There are five effects you can add to your text:
  - **Upside down** (see the following illustration):

Regular   Upside down

- **Backwards**, which is used to write from right to left:

Regular   Backwards

- **Width Factor**, which affects the width/height:

Regular   Width Factor = 1.50   Width Factor = 0.75

- **Oblique Angle** (see the following):

Regular   Oblique Angle = +15   Oblique Angle = -15

- **Vertical** is only applicable for **.shx* fonts—it will write the text from top to bottom (good for any **.shx* Chinese fonts).
- When you are done, click the **Apply** button, and then the **Close** button.
- At the left part of the dialog box, there is a pop-up list showing **All styles**. Depending upon your specifications, this list will show you all of the defined text styles—whether they are used or not used—or only the text styles that are used in the current drawing.

CREATING TEXT STYLES (METRIC)

Workshop 12-A

1. Start AutoCAD 2010.
2. Open the file *Workshop_12.dwg*.
3. Create a text style named "Title" with the following settings:
   a. **Font** = Arial
   b. **Font Style** = Bold
   c. **Height** = 900
   d. **Width Factor** = 2
4. Create a text style named "Inside_Annot" with the following settings:
   a. **Font** = Times New Roman
   b. **Font Style** = Regular
   c. **Height** = 300
   d. **Width Factor** = 1
5. Create a text style named "Dimension" with the following settings:
   a. **Font** = Arial
   b. **Font Style** = Regular
   c. **Height** = 400
   d. **Width Factor** = 1
6. Save the file and close it.

CREATING TEXT STYLES (IMPERIAL)

Workshop 12-B

1. Start AutoCAD 2010.
2. Open the file *Workshop_12.dwg*.
3. Create a text style named "Title" with the following settings:
   a. **Font** = Arial
   b. **Font Style** = Bold
   c. **Height** = 3'-0"
   d. **Width Factor** = 2
4. Create a text style named "Inside_Annot" with the following settings:
   a. **Font** = Times New Roman
   b. **Font Style** = Regular
   c. **Height** = 1'-0"
   d. **Width Factor** = 1
5. Create a text style named "Dimension" with the following settings:
   a. **Font** = Arial
   b. **Font Style** = Regular
   c. **Height** = 1'-4"
   d. **Width Factor** = 1
6. Save the file and close it.

8.3 SINGLE LINE TEXT

- **Single Line Text** is the first of two commands you can use to write text in AutoCAD.
- Although you write several lines of text in each command, each line would be considered a separate object.
- To start the **Single Line Text** command, make sure you are in the **Annotate** tab on the **Ribbon**, and, using the **Text** panel, select the **Single Line** button:

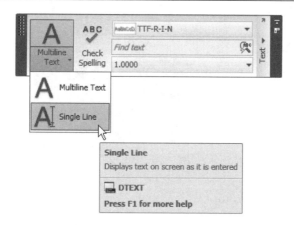

- The following prompt will appear:

```
Current text style:  "arial_09"  Text height:
0.9000  Annotative No
Specify start point of text or [Justify/Style]:
(Specify the start point of the baseline)
Specify rotation angle of text <0>: (Specify the rotation
angle of the baseline, then press [Enter] and start writing)
```

- You will see the text on the screen. Press [Enter] once each time you want a new line; press [Enter] twice to end the command.
- As previously noted, AutoCAD will use the current text style to write the desired text. In the **Text** panel, you will see something like the following:

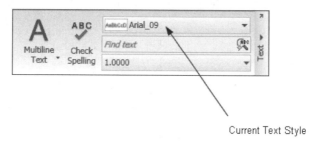

Current Text Style

8.4 MULTILINE TEXT

- The **Multiline Text** command simulates Microsoft® Word simplicity in creating text. It is easier for people who have experience using Word.
- All the text you write in a single command would be considered a single object.
- To start the **Multiline Text** command, make sure you are in the **Home** tab on the **Ribbon**, and, using the **Annotation** panel, select the **Multiline Text** button.

- The following prompt will appear:

```
Current text style:  "arial_09"  Text height:  0.9000
Annotative  No
Specify first corner: (Specify first corner)
Specify opposite corner or [Height/Justify/Line spacing/
Rotation/Style/Width]: (Specify opposite corner)
```

- At the first prompt, the cursor will change to a crosshair:

- After you specify the first point, you will get something like the following:

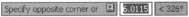

- AutoCAD wants you to select two opposite corners to specify the area that you will write in.
- After you specify the two corners, a text editor with a ruler will appear:

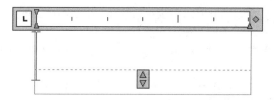

- AutoCAD will automatically present a new tab called **Text Editor** (that will disappear when you are done with this command), which looks like the following:

- A blinking cursor will appear in the text editor so you can type your desired text. Using the **Text Editor** tab, you can format the text as you wish.
- If you created a text style (highly recommended), then at the left part of the tab you will see the name of the current text style along with the height.
- In order to format any text, you should select it first just as you would in Microsoft Word.

Formatting Panel

- The **Formatting** panel is as follows:

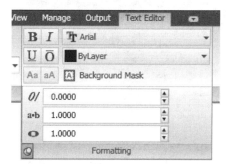

- Use the **Formatting** panel to change any or all of the following:
  - Change the text to be **Bold**.
  - Change the text to be **Italic**.
  - Change the text to be **Underlined**.
  - Change the text to be **Overlined**.

- Change the font (it is recommended to stick with the font specified by the current text style).
- Change the color of the text (it is recommended to stick with the color of the current layer).
- Convert an uppercase letter to a lowercase letter, and vice versa.
- Specify the **Background Mask** (the background color). You will see the following dialog box:

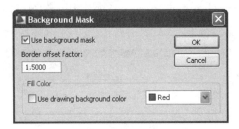

- Specify the **Oblique Angle**.
- Specify the **Tracking** to increase or decrease the spaces between letters. Values greater than 1 mean more space between letters, and vice versa.
- Specify the **Width Factor**.

Paragraph Panel

- The **Paragraph** panel is as follows:

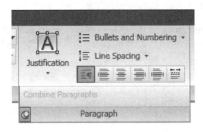

- Use the **Paragraph** panel to change any or all of the following: **Justification**, **Bullets and Numbering**, and **Line Spacing**.
  - Change the **Justification** to one of the following nine options:

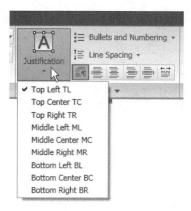

- To understand **Justification**, look at the following illustration:

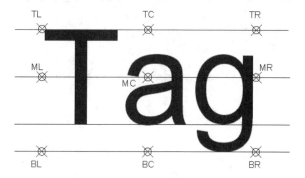

- You can use **Bullets and Numbering**, where you can choose between using letters (lowercase or uppercase), numbers, or bullets.

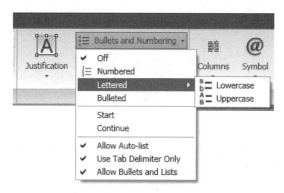

- You can set the **Line Spacing** of the paragraph. You have the choice of 1.0x, 1.5x, 2.0x, 2.5x, or you can set your own.

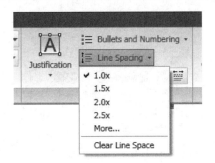

- You can change the justification of the paragraph by using the six justification buttons as illustrated:

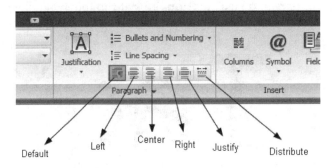

Insert Panel

- The **Insert** panel is as follows:

- You can add **Symbols** to your text. If you click the **Symbol** button, the following menu will appear. You can add one of 20 available symbols:

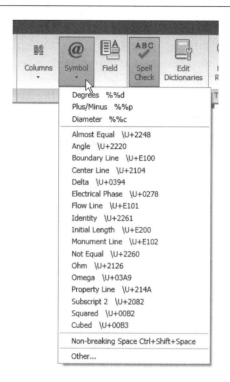

Spell Check Panel

- The **Spell Check** panel is as follows:

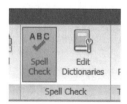

- By default, the **Spell Check** button is on. While you are typing, a dotted red line will appear under the misspelled words, just like the following example:

- Go to the misspelled word and right-click. Suggestions for the correct spelling will appear at the top of the shortcut menu. If you need more suggestions, you can see them in a submenu, as shown in the following:

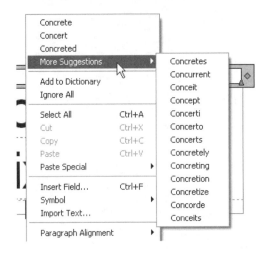

- To use other dictionaries, click the **Edit Dictionaries** button. You will see the following dialog box:

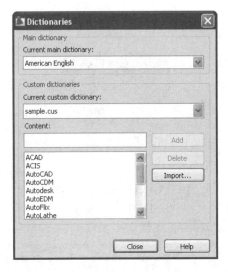

Tools Panel

- The **Tools** panel is as follows:

- In the **Tools** panel, you can **Find and Replace** text, **Import Text**, and use the **AuotCAPS** button.
  - Click the **Find and Replace** button and the following dialog box will appear:

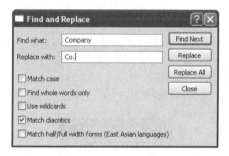

  - You can replace one or all of the occurrences.
  - You can use the **Import Text** button to place text already stored as a text file. The following dialog box will appear:

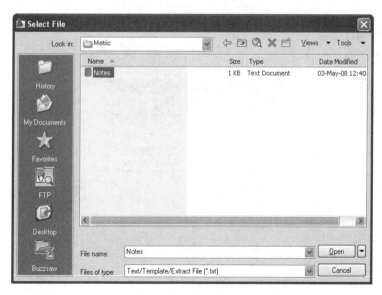

- Select the desired drive and folder, and then select the desired *.txt* file. Once you click **Open**, you will see the text in the editor available for formatting.
- Use the **AutoCAPS** button to write in uppercase letters (just like using **Caps Lock** on the keyboard).

Options Panel

- The **Options** panel is as follows:

- Using the **Options** panel, you can do any or all of the following:
  - **Undo** any mistake you make while typing or **redo** it
  - **Show** or **Hide** the ruler
  - Show more options (see the following):

Character Set

- To choose a different character set, select from the submenu:

Remove Formatting

- In order for **Remove Formatting** to be active, you have to select the text first. AutoCAD will give you the ability to remove the formatting on the selected text:

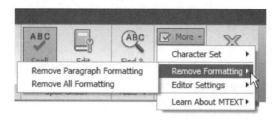

Editor Settings

- To control the **Editor Settings**, choose from the submenu:

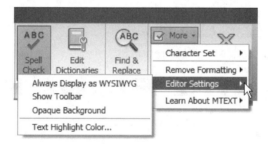

Close Panel

- The **Close** panel enables you to close the **Text Editor** tab:

Set Indents

- Setting indents in the **Text Editor** is identical to the process in Microsoft Word. See the following illustration:

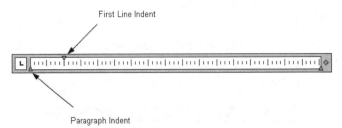

- Move the **First Line Indent** to specify where the first line will start.
- Move the **Paragraph Indent** to specify where the next line will start.
- Also, you can set **Tabs** for your text by clicking anywhere in the ruler.

WRITING TEXT (METRIC AND IMPERIAL)

 Workshops 13-A and 13-B
1. Start AutoCAD 2010.
2. Open the file *Workshop_13.dwg*.
3. Review the following illustration:

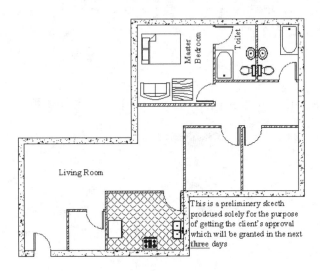

4. Make the **Text** layer the current layer.
5. Using **Single Line Text** (**DTEXT** command) and the text style "Inside_Annot," type the following words: **Master Bedroom, Toilet, Living Room**.

6. Using **Single Line Text** (**DTEXT** command) and the text style "Title," type the following words: **Ground Floor Plan**.

7. Switch off the **OSNAP** button.

8. Using the **Multiline Text** command, specify the area in the lower right-hand part of the plan as previously shown. Using the text style "Inside_Annot," import the file named *Notes.txt*. Don't close the text editor.

9. Select the word **three**, and make it red, bold, and underlined. Close the editor.

10. Save the file and close it.

8.5 AN INTRODUCTION TO EDITING TEXT

- In order to edit the contents of the text, simply double-click the text.
- If you double-click multiline text, the editor will reappear with the **Multiline Text** tab. You can use this tab for further adding, deleting, or reformatting.
- If you double-click single line text, the text will be available for adding and deleting.
- Also, you can select multiline text, right-click, and select **Mtext Edit**.

8.6 EDITING TEXT USING QUICK PROPERTIES AND PROPERTIES

Single Line Text

- In order to edit the properties of single line text, simply click it. The **Quick Properties** window will appear and you can make changes like the following:

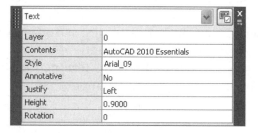

- You can change the **Layer**, **Contents**, **Style**, **Annotative** status, **Justification**, **Height**, and finally, the **Rotation** angle.
- If you want to do more editing, select **Properties**, and you will see the following:

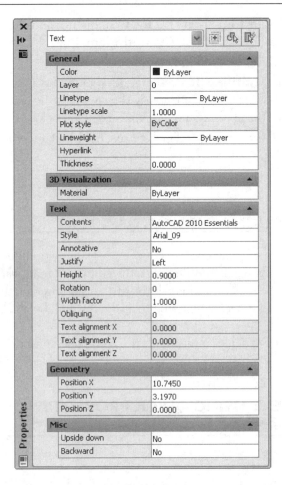

- You can change the **General** properties of the single line text (**Color**, **Layer**, **Linetype**, etc.).
- You can change the **Contents** of the text and other properties, such as **Style**, **Justification**, **Height**, **Rotation**, etc.).
- You can change the **Geometry** of the text (position of **X**, **Y**, and **Z**).
- Finally, you can change the **Miscellaneous** properties of single line text to **Upside down** and/or **Backward**.

Multiline Text

- In order to edit the properties of multiline text, simply click it. The **Quick Properties** window will appear and you can make changes as shown in the following:

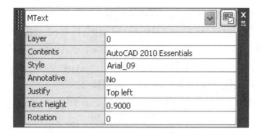

- You can edit the same things you can change in single line text.
- In order to have full editing power, you need to start the **Properties** command. You will see the following:

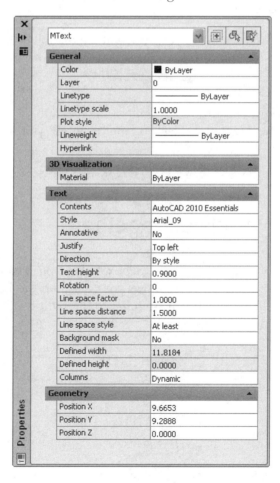

- You can change the **General** properties of the multiline text (**Color**, **Layer**, **Linetype**, etc.)

- You can change the **Contents** of the multiline text and other properties like **Style**, **Justification**, **Direction**, **Height**, **Rotation**, etc.
- You can change the specific features of multiline text like the **Line space factor**, **Line space distance**, **Line space style**, **Background mask**, **Defined width**, and **Defined height**.
- NOTE 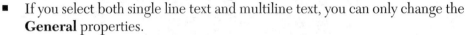 If you select both single line text and multiline text, you can only change the **General** properties.
- You can select either multiple single line text or multiple multiline text and change their properties in one step.

8.7 TEXT AND GRIPS

- If you click on single line text, you will see the following:

Elevation

- The grip appears at the start point of the baseline.
- On the other hand, if you click on multiline text, you will see the following:

Elevations and Cross
Sections will be
modified together

- You will see a grip at the top left, which will allow you to move the multiline text.
- The arrow at the top right allows you to extend the horizontal dimension of the multiline text. If you stretch it to the right it will increase and if you stretch it to left it will decrease.

Elevations
and Cross
Sections
will be
modified
together

- The arrow at the bottom will place the text in multiple columns:

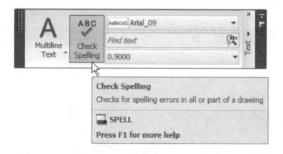

8.8 CHECK SPELLING AND FIND AND REPLACE

Check Spelling

- We have already learned how to **Spell Check** and **Find and Replace** inside the multiline text editor. But what if we want to check an existing single line or multiline text? We can use two tools.
- AutoCAD will spell check the entire drawing, the current space/layout, or selected text.
- To start the **Check Spelling** command, make sure you are in the **Annotate** tab on the **Ribbon**, and, using the **Text** panel, select the **Check Spelling** button.

- The following dialog box will appear:

- This is identical to the spell checker in Microsoft Word. If AutoCAD finds a misspelled word, it will give you suggestions and you can choose one of them. You can also change or ignore the suggestion.

Find and Replace

- AutoCAD can find any word or part of a word in the entire drawing file and replace it.
- To start the **Find and Replace** command, make sure you are in the **Annotate** tab on the **Ribbon**, and, using the **Text** panel, type the desired word in the ***Find text*** field:

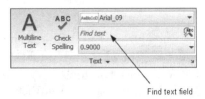

Find text field

- Type the word or phrase you are looking for in the edit box and click the key at the right. AutoCAD will locate the word and show the following dialog box:

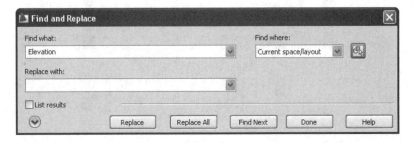

- Under **Replace with**, type the new word(s) you want to appear in place of the word(s) given in **Find what**.
- You can search the entire drawing or search in a selection of text.
- You have three choices: **Find**, **Replace**, and **Replace All**.
- When you are finished, click **Done**.

EDITING TEXT (METRIC AND IMPERIAL)

Workshops 14-A and 14-B
1. Start AutoCAD 2010.
2. Open the file *Workshop_14.dwg*.

3. Select the multiline text and the four grips will appear. Select one of the right grips to make it hot and stretch it to the right to make the text one line less.

4. Double-click the multiline text and make the following changes:

    a. Select the word "solely" and make it italic.

    b. Add a comma before the word "which."

    c. Press [Enter] after the last word to add a new line and type your initials.

5. While you are in the text editor, you can see three words with dashed red lines beneath them. Use the **Check Spelling** command for these three words and select the correct spelling.

6. Save the file and close it.

8.9 TABLE STYLE

- To create a table in AutoCAD, perform the following two steps:
  - Create a table style.
  - **Insert** and **Fill** the table.
- In **Table Style** you will define the main features of your table.
- To start the **Table Style** command, make sure you are in the **Home** tab on the **Ribbon**, and, expanding the **Annotation** panel, click the **Table Style** button:

- You will see the following dialog box:

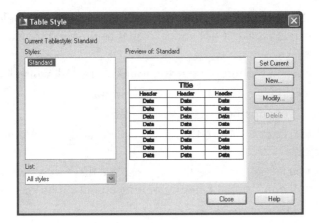

- As you can see, there is a predefined style called **Standard**.
- There will always be a preview that will show you the changes you are making. Therefore, it will be easy for you to decide if you have made the right choices.
- To create a new table style, click the **New** button. You will see the following dialog box:

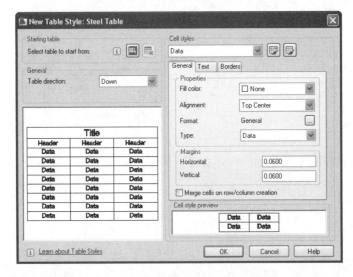

- Type in the name of your new style.
- Select the **Start With** style (you will start with a copy from this style).
- Click the **Continue** button. The following dialog box will appear:

- Under **Starting table**, you can select an existing table and copy its style instead of starting from scratch.

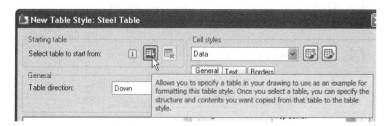

- Under **General**, specify the **Table direction**:
  - **Down**: The title and column headers will be located at the top of the table and the cells will go below them.
  - **Up**: The title and column headers will be located at the bottom of the table and the cells will go above them.
- Under **Cell styles**, you have three choices: **Data**, **Header**, and **Title**. This feature controls the table's three parts.

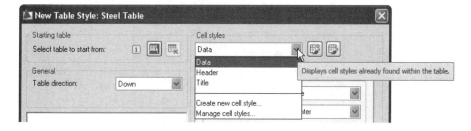

- You can control the **General** properties, **Text** properties, and **Border** properties of these three parts.

General Tab

- The **General** properties tab looks like the following:

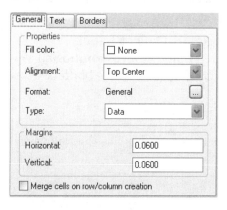

- Set the **Fill Color**, **Alignment**, **Format**, **Type**, and **Margins**.
  - **Fill Color**: Determine whether the cells will have a colored background.
  - **Alignment**: Determine the justification of the text compared to the cell (you have nine to choose from). To illustrate the last two options, see the following example:

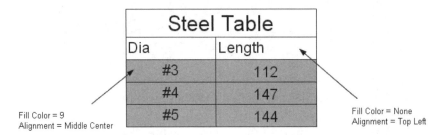

Fill Color = 9
Alignment = Middle Center

Fill Color = None
Alignment = Top Left

  - **Format**: Select the format of the numbers. Click on the small button with the three dots and you will see the following dialog box:

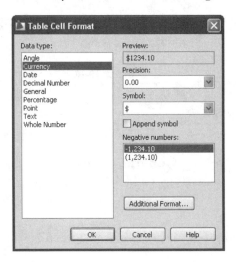

  - Set the **Type** to be **Data** or **Label**.
  - **Margins**: Determine the **Horizontal** and **Vertical** distances to be taken around the **Data** relative to the borders.

Text Tab

- The **Text** properties tab looks like the following:

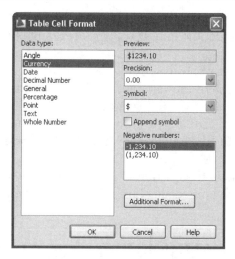

- In the **Text** tab, you can control the following settings:
  - The text style you will use in the cells.
  - The text height to be used (this is only applicable if the selected text style has a Height = 0).
  - The text color to be used (you should most likely leave it **ByLayer** or **ByBlock**).
  - The text angle sets the oblique angle of the text.

Borders Tab

- The **Borders** properties tab looks like the following:

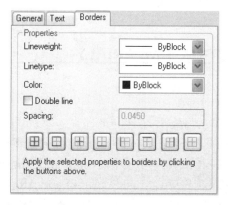

- In the **Borders** tab, you can control the following settings:
  - Specify the **Lineweight**, **Linetype**, and **Color** of the borders (either choose **ByBlock** or specify the desired value from the list).

- Specify whether you want the border to be single line (the default setting) or double line. If you specify double line, you must also specify the spacing.
- Set the type of border (inside, outside, etc.).
■ Once you set all of the variables, click **OK** to go back to the first dialog box and do any or all of the following:
  - Select the current style from many available styles. The selected style becomes the default, which you will see the next time you use the **Table** command.
  - Select one of the existing styles and make any type of modification; you will see the same dialog box you see when you create a new style.

CREATING TABLE STYLE (METRIC)

Workshop 15-A
1. Start AutoCAD 2010.
2. Open the file *Workshop_15.dwg*.
3. Create a new table style based on **Standard** and call it **Door Schedule**.
    a. For title, **Text Style** = Inside_Annot and **Alignment** = Middle Center.
    b. For data, **Text Style** = Inside_Annot and **Alignment** = Middle Center.
    c. For header, **Text Style** = Inside_Annot and **Alignment** = Middle Center.
    d. For cell margins, **Horizontal** = 100 and **Vertical** = 100.
4. Make it current.
5. Save the file and close it.

CREATING TABLE STYLE (IMPERIAL)

Workshop 15-B
1. Start AutoCAD 2010.
2. Open the file *Workshop_15.dwg*.
3. Create a new table style based on **Standard** and call it **Door Schedule**.
    a. For title, **Text Style** = Inside_Annot and **Alignment** = Middle Center.
    b. For data, **Text Style** = Inside_Annot and **Alignment** = Middle Center.
    c. For header, **Text Style** = Inside_Annot and **Alignment** = Middle Center.
    d. For cell margins, **Horizontal** = 4" and **Vertical** = 4"
4. Make it current.
5. Save the file and close it.

8.10 THE TABLE COMMAND

- Use the **Table** command to insert a table in an AutoCAD drawing using a predefined style.
- You will specify the number of columns and rows, and fill the cells with the desired data.
- To start the **Table** command, make sure you are in the **Home** tab on the **Ribbon**, and, using the **Annotation** panel, click the **Table** button.

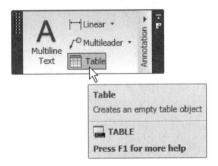

- The following dialog box will appear:

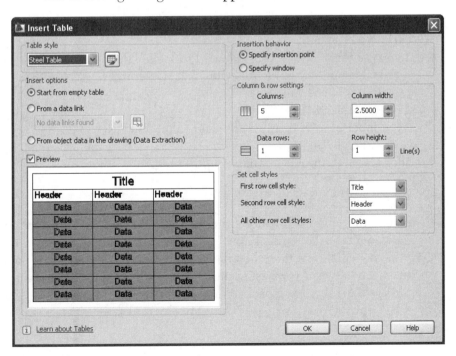

- Select the predefined **Table style** name.
- If you did not create a table style before this step, simply click the small button next to the list, so you can start creating the desired table style.

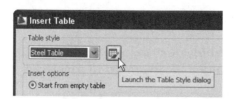

- Specify the **Insert options**. You have three choices:
  - Start from an empty table—normally, this option should be used.
  - Import from a data link—to bring in data from spreadsheets created in an application like Microsoft® Excel.
  - Import from object data in the drawing (**Data Extraction**)—use only if you have block attributes.
- There are two insertion methods:
  - Specify insertion point
  - Specify window

Specify Insertion Point

- If you use this method, you will need to specify the upper left-hand corner of the table and set up the following data accordingly:
  - Number of columns
  - Column width
  - Number of rows (without title and column heads)
  - Row height (in lines)
- Click **OK** and AutoCAD will prompt:

```
Specify insertion point:
```

- Specify the upper left-hand corner of the table and the table will appear ready to fill the data in each row.
- First you will fill the title, then the column headers, and then the data. You can move between rows using the [Tab] key to go to the next cell and the [Shift]+[Tab] keys to go back to the previous cell.

Specify Window

- If you use this method, you will be asked later to specify a window. You must specify a total height and a total width.

- If you specify the number of columns, the column width will be calculated automatically (total width/number of columns). Or, it you specify the column width, the number of columns will be calculated automatically (total width/single column width).
- The same thing applies to rows. Either specify the number of rows, and the row height will be calculated automatically (total height/number of rows), or specify the row height, and the number of rows will be calculated automatically (total height/single row height).

- Click **OK** and AutoCAD will prompt:

```
Specify first corner:
Specify second corner:
```

- Specify two opposite corners and the table will be available for input just like the previous method.

 - To edit cell content, simply double-click the cell and it will be available for editing.

INSERTING TABLES (METRIC)

 Workshop 16-A
1. Start AutoCAD 2010.
2. Open the file *Workshop_16.dwg.*
3. Make the **Text** layer the current layer.
4. Look at the following illustration. Using the **Door Schedule** table style, add a table just like the one here, using the following:
   a. Specify insertion point
   b. **Columns** = 5
   c. **Column Width** = 2000
   d. **Data Rows** = 4
   e. **Row Height** = 1 Line(s)

Ground Floor Plan

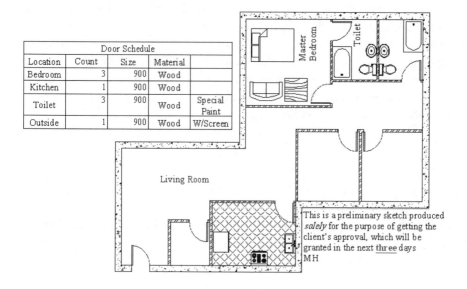

Door Schedule				
Location	Count	Size	Material	
Bedroom	3	900	Wood	
Kitchen	1	900	Wood	
Toilet	3	900	Wood	Special Paint
Outside	1	900	Wood	W/Screen

Master Bedroom

Toilet

Living Room

This is a preliminary sketch produced *solely* for the purpose of getting the client's approval, which will be granted in the next three days MH

5. Save the file and close it.

INSERTING TABLES (IMPERIAL)

Workshop 16-B

1. Start AutoCAD 2010.
2. Open the file *Workshop_16.dwg*.
3. Make the **Text** layer the current layer.
4. Look at the following illustration. Using the **Door Schedule** table style, add a table just like the one here, using the following:
    a. Specify insertion point.
    b. **Columns** = 5
    c. **Column Width** = 6'-8"
    d. **Data Rows** = 4
    e. **Row Height** = 1 Line(s)

Ground Floor Plan

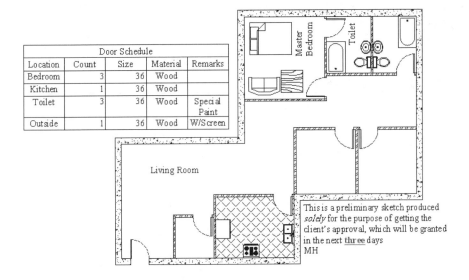

Door Schedule				
Location	Count	Size	Material	Remarks
Bedroom	3	36	Wood	
Kitchen	1	36	Wood	
Toilet	3	36	Wood	Special Paint
Outside	1	36	Wood	W/Screen

Master Bedroom

Toilet

Living Room

This is a preliminary sketch produced *solely* for the purpose of getting the client's approval, which will be granted in the next three days
MH

5.   Save the file and close it.

CHAPTER REVIEW

1.   The height mentioned in the **Text Style** is for lowercase letters.
   a. True
   b. False

2.   There are two types of fonts in AutoCAD: _____ and _____.

3.   There is no relation between **Text style** and **Table style**.
   a. True
   b. False

4.   While you are in the **multiline text editor** you can't:
   a. Import any *.txt* files.
   b. Format text.
   c. Change the indents.
   d. Bring in a Microsoft Word document as OLE.

5.   Which one of the following statements is not true about tables?
   a. There are two methods to insert a table.
   b. You can control the cell style for title, header, and data.

     c. You can convert multiline text to a table.

     d. You can define the table direction whether it is down or top.

6. In **Table style**, Top, Left, and Middle are considered to be _____ options.

CHAPTER REVIEW ANSWERS

1. b
2. *.shx, .ttf*
3. b
4. d
5. c
6. **Justification**

Chapter **9**

Dimensioning Your Drawing

In This Chapter

- ◊ Introduction
- ◊ Dimension Types
- ◊ **Dimension Style**: The First Step
- ◊ The **Lines** Tab
- ◊ The **Symbols and Arrows** Tab
- ◊ The **Text** Tab
- ◊ The **Fit** Tab
- ◊ The **Primary Units** Tab
- ◊ The **Alternate Units** Tab
- ◊ The **Tolerances** Tab
- ◊ Creating a Sub Style
- ◊ Controlling **Dimension Styles**
- ◊ An Introduction to Dimensioning Commands
- ◊ The **Linear** Command
- ◊ The **Aligned** Command
- ◊ The **Angular** Command
- ◊ The **Arc Length** Command
- ◊ The **Radius** Command
- ◊ The **Diameter** Command
- ◊ The **Jogged** Command
- ◊ The **Ordinate** Command
- ◊ The **Continue** Command
- ◊ The **Baseline** Command
- ◊ The **Quick Dimension** Command
- ◊ Dimension Blocks and Grips
- ◊ Dimension Block Properties
- ◊ An Introduction to the Multileader
- ◊ Multileader: Creating the Style
- ◊ **Multileader** Commands

9.1 INTRODUCTION

- Dimensioning in AutoCAD® is a semi-automatic process; users contribute part of the job and AutoCAD does the rest.
- Users in linear dimensioning, for example, specify three points. The first and the second is the length to be dimensioned, and the third is the position of the dimension line.
- Accordingly, AutoCAD will generate the **Dimension block** automatically, as shown in the following illustration:

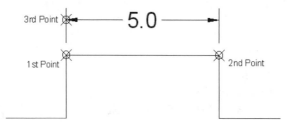

- A **Dimension block** consists of four parts. They are:
  - Dimension line
  - Extension lines
  - Arrowheads
  - Dimension text
- See the following illustration:

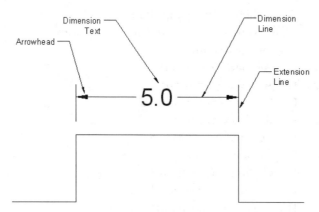

- The Dimensioning process has two phases:
  - Creating dimension style(s)
  - Dimensioning your drawing
- The dimension style will control the appearance of the **Dimension block**. Each user will set up the style according to their needs.

- Creating a dimension style is a lengthy and tedious job, but it will be done only once, thereby allowing users to focus on the other job of putting dimensions over the drawing.

9.2 DIMENSION TYPES

- AutoCAD can support the following dimension types:
  - Linear and Aligned
  - Arc Length, Radius, and Diameter
  - Angular
  - Continuous
  - Baseline
  - Ordinate

Linear and Aligned

- See the following illustration:

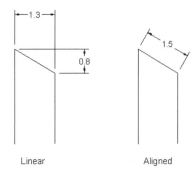

Linear   Aligned

Arc Length, Radius, and Diameter

- See the following illustration:

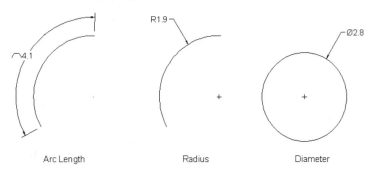

Arc Length   Radius   Diameter

Angular

- See the following illustration:

Angular

Continuous

- See the following illustration:

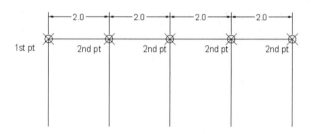

Baseline

- See the following illustration:

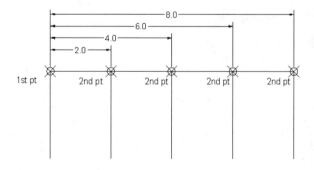

Ordinate

- See the following illustration:

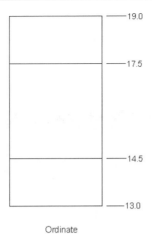

Ordinate

9.3 DIMENSION STYLE: THE FIRST STEP

- To start the **Dimension Style** command, make sure you are in the **Home** tab on the **Ribbon**, and, expanding the **Annotation** panel, click the **Dimension Style** button.

- The following dialog box will appear:

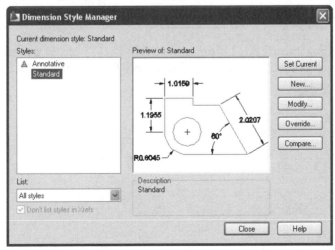

- By default, there is a template for the dimension style called **Standard**.
- You can modify this style or create your own (which is the more preferable choice).
- To create a new style, click the **New** button. The following dialog box will appear:

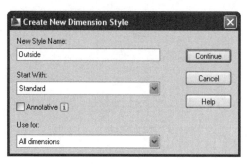

- Type in a new style name using the same naming convention you used when creating layers.
- Select the **Start With** style (you will start with a copy of this style).
- Keep **Annotative** off for now.
- By default, the changes you will make will be implemented for all types of dimensions. However, you can also create a new dimension style that will affect a certain type of dimension.
- Click the **Continue** button and begin modifying the settings. We will cover each tab of the **Dimension Style** dialog box in the coming pages.
- NOTE ▶ Whenever you find a **Color** setting, leave it as is. It is preferable to control colors through layers and not through individual objects. This also applies for **Linetype** and **Lineweight**.

9.4 THE LINES TAB

- The first tab in the **Dimension Style** dialog box is **Lines**. This is where we will control **Dimension lines** and **Extension lines**. It looks like the following:

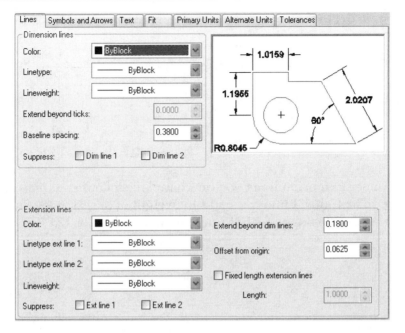

- You can control the following settings under **Dimension lines**:
  - The **Color**, **Linetype**, and **Lineweight** of the dimension line.
  - **Extend beyond ticks** (to edit this value, go to the **Symbols and Arrows** tab and set the **Arrowhead** to be either **Architectural tick** or **Oblique**). See the following illustration:

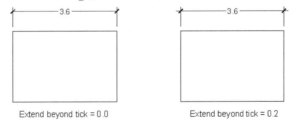

- See the following illustration for **Baseline spacing**:

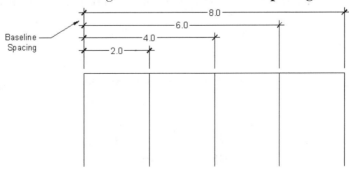

- Select to **Suppress Dim line 1** for one of them or **Dim line 2** for both:

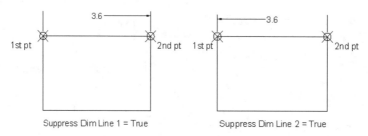

- Under **Extension lines**, you can control the following settings:
  - The **Color**, **Linetype**, and **Lineweight** of the extension lines.
  - Select to **Suppress Ext line 1** for one of them or **Ext line 2** for both:

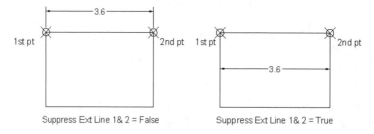

- Specify **Extend beyond dim lines** and **Offset from origin**:

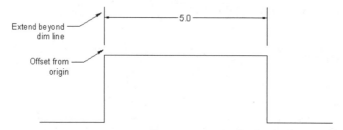

- In order to set **Fixed length extension lines**, you have to specify the **Length**. See the following example for a better understanding:

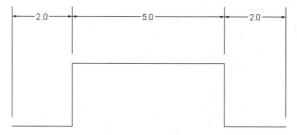

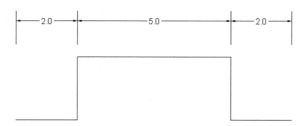

Fixed length extension lines = on & Length = 1.00

 ■ The **Length** you specify will be calculated from the dimension origin up to the dimension line.

9.5 THE SYMBOLS AND ARROWS TAB

■ When you click on the **Symbols and Arrows** tab, you will see the following:

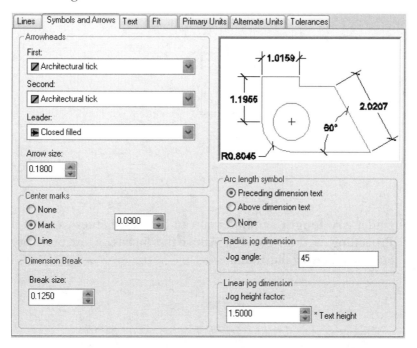

■ Under **Arrowheads**, you can control the following settings:
- The shape of the **First** arrowhead.
- The shape of the **Second** arrowhead.
- The shape of the arrowhead to be used in the **Leader**.
- The **Size** of the arrowhead.

- If you change the first, the second will change automatically, but if you change the second, the first will not change.
- Under **Center marks**, you can:
  - Select whether or not to show the center mark or the centerlines.
  - Set the **Size** of the center mark.

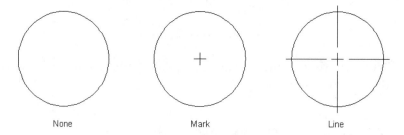

- Under **Dimension Break**, set the **Break size**. This is the width of the break of the dimension lines in a dimension break.

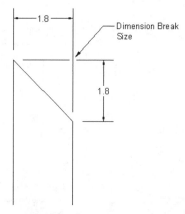

- Under **Arc length symbol**, you can decide whether to show the symbol **Preceding** the dimension text, **Above** the dimension text, or not at all (**None**). See the following illustration:

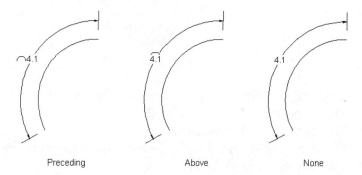

- Under **Radius jog dimension**, set the value of the **Jog angle**:

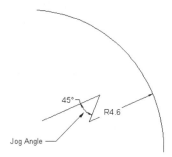

- Under **Linear jog dimension**, set the **Jog height factor** as a percentage of the text height. See the following illustration:

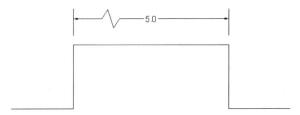

Jog height factor = 3 times the height of text

9.6 THE TEXT TAB

- When you click on the **Text** tab, you will see the following:

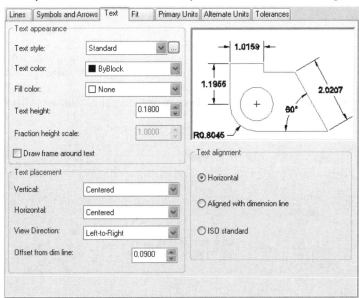

- Under **Text appearance**, you can control the following settings by:
  - Selecting the desired premade **Text style** to be used to input the dimension text. If you did not create a text style prior to this step, you can click the button with the three dots and create it now.
  - Specifying the **Text color**.
  - Specifying the **Fill color** (the background color).

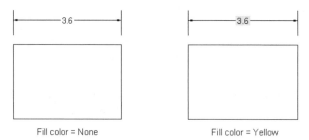

Fill color = None   Fill color = Yellow

  - Inputting the **Text height** (only applicable if the assigned text style has a text height = 0.0).
  - Going to the **Primary Units** tab and assigning the **Unit format** to be **Architectural** or **Fractional**. Then, the dimension text will appear close to 1 1/4. You can set the **Fraction height scale** if you would like the text set at a different height.
  - Deciding whether or not to **Draw frame around** the dimension text.

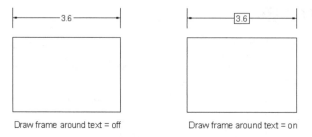

Draw frame around text = off   Draw frame around text = on

- As an introduction to **Text placement**, see the following illustration:

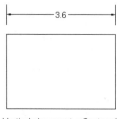

Vertical placement = Centered
Horizontal placement = Centered

- Under **Text placement**, you can:
  - Select the **Vertical** placement. You have five choices: **Centered**, **Above**, **Outside**, **JIS** (Japan Industrial Standard), and **Below**. See the following illustration:

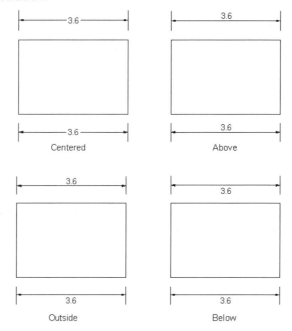

- Select the **Horizontal** placement. You have five choices: **Centered**, **At Ext Line 1**, **At Ext Line 2**, **Over Ext Line 1**, and **Over Ext Line 2**. See the following illustration:

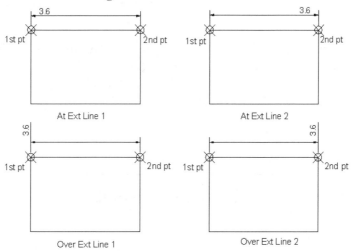

- Set the **View Direction** of the dimension text to be either **Left-to-Right** or **Right-to-Left**.
- Set the **Offset from dim line**, which is the distance between the dimension line and the baseline of the dimension text. See the following illustration:

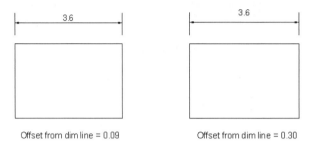

Offset from dim line = 0.09   Offset from dim line = 0.30

- Under **Text alignment**, control whether the text will always be **Horizontal**, **Aligned with dimension line**, or according to **ISO standard**. See the following illustration:

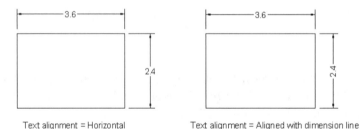

Text alignment = Horizontal   Text alignment = Aligned with dimension line

NOTE
- The only difference between **Aligned with dimension line** and **ISO standard** is the **Radius** and **Diameter** types. The first is considered, like the other types, to be aligned with the dimension line, and **ISO standard** is considered to be horizontal.

9.7 THE FIT TAB

- When you click on the **Fit** tab, you will see the following:

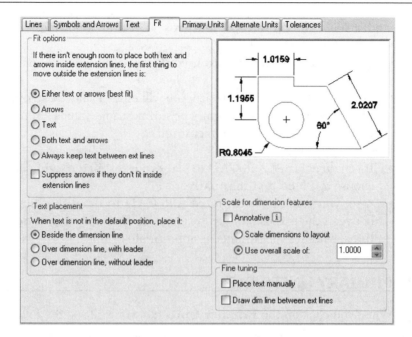

- As an introduction to the **Fit** tab, notice that there are three things that will be within the two extension lines: the **Dimension line, Arrowheads**, and the **Dimension text**. AutoCAD will put them all inside the two extension lines when the distance can accommodate all three. What if there is not enough room? We will discuss that option here.
- Under **Fit options**, adjust the following settings:
  - Select one of the five options to decide how AutoCAD will treat **Arrowheads** and **Dimension text**.
  - Select whether to **Suppress arrows if they don't fit inside extension lines** or not.
- Under **Text placement**, control the placement of the text. If it does not fit inside the extension lines, you have three options: **Beside the dimension line**, **Over dimension line with leader**, and **Over dimension line without leader**. See the following illustration:

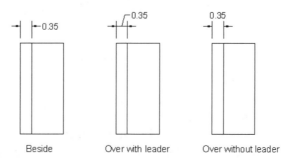

- Under **Scale for dimension features**, adjust the following:
  - Keep **Annotative** off for now.
  - Set the **Scale dimension to layout** (we will discuss layouts in the next chapter).
  - For any distance, length, or size, you will input a value. **Use overall scale of** is a setting that will magnify or shrink whole values in one step. This will not affect the distance measured.
- Under **Fine tuning**:
  - If you do not trust AutoCAD to place your text in the right place, you can choose to **Place text manually**.
  - Also, you can choose to force AutoCAD to draw the dimension line between the extension lines by choosing **Draw dim line between ext lines**, whether the distance is appropriate or not.

9.8 THE PRIMARY UNITS TAB

- When you click on the **Primary Units** tab, you will see the following:

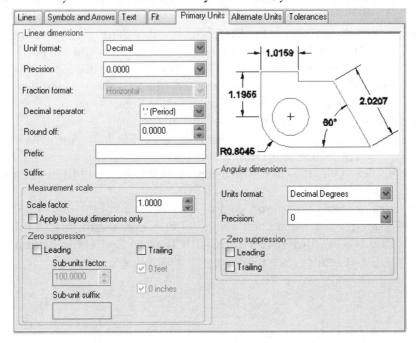

- As an introduction to the **Primary Units**, let us assume that your client wants the dimensions in Decimal format and a subcontractor wants it in Architectural format. The solution will be to show two numbers for each dimension, where the first will be the **Primary Units** and the second will be the **Alternate Units**. In this section we will cover the **Primary Units**.

- Under **Linear dimensions**:
  - Choose the **Unit format** and select one of the six available formats.
  - Select the **Precision** of the unit format selected.
  - If you select the Architectural or Fractional format, specify the **Fraction format**, which includes **Horizontal**, **Diagonal**, and **Not Stacked**.
  - If you select **Decimal**, specify the **Decimal Separator—Period**, **Comma**, or **Space**.
  - Specify the **Round off** number. If you select 0.5, for example, then AutoCAD will round off any dimension to the nearest 0.5.
  - Input the **Prefix** and/or the **Suffix**. See the following illustration for a better understanding.

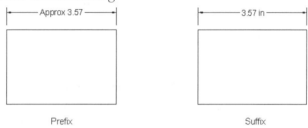

- Under **Measurement scale**:
  - Input the **Scale factor**. To understand the importance of this setting, let's assume we have a drawing that uses the millimeter as the unit—hence a length of 10 m will be 10,000—but we want the value 10 to appear and not 10,000. To do so, we set the **Scale factor** to be 0.001.
  - Select **Apply to layout dimensions only** (we will discuss the layouts in the next chapter).
- Under **Zero suppression**, select to suppress the **Leading**, and/or the **Trailing** zeros. See the following illustration:

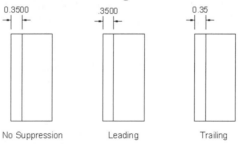

- If you have meters as your unit, and the measured value is less then one centimeter, we call this a sub unit. Set up the **Sub-units factor** (in our example 1 m = 100 cm, so the factor = 100) and the suffix for it.
- Under **Angular dimensions**, select the **Unit format** and the **Precision**.
- Under **Zero suppression**, select to suppress the **Leading** and/or the **Trailing** zeros for the angular measurements.

9.9 THE ALTERNATE UNITS TAB

- When you click on the **Alternate Units** tab, you will see the following:

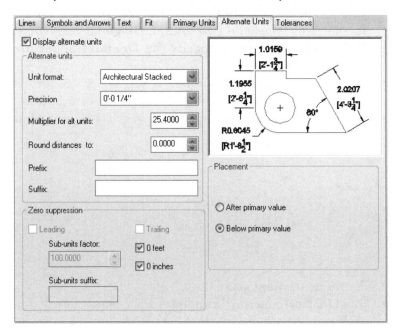

- If you want two numbers to appear for each dimension, click on **Display alternate units**.
- Specify the alternate **Unit format**, its **Precision**, the **Multiplier for all units** value, the **Round distances to**, the **Prefix**, the **Suffix**, and the **Zero suppression** criteria.
- Specify whether to show the alternate units **After primary value** or **Below primary value**. See the following illustration:

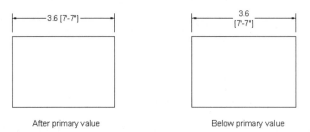

After primary value   Below primary value

9.10 THE TOLERANCES TAB

- When you click on the **Tolerances** tab, you will see the following:

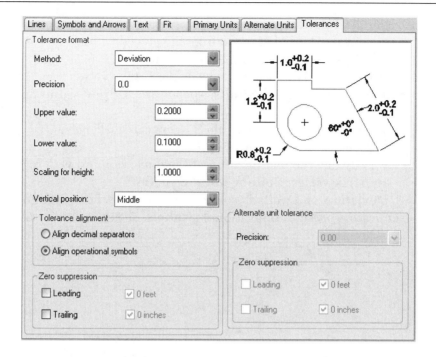

- There are several ways to show the tolerances, they are:
  - **Symmetrical**
  - **Deviation**
  - **Limits**
  - **Basic**
- See the following illustration:

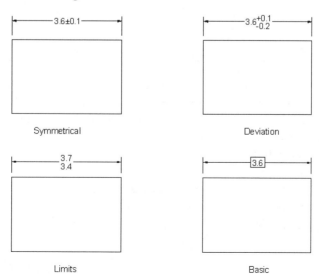

- Under the **Tolerance format**:
  - Specify the desired **Method** from the preceding list.
  - Specify the **Precision** of the numbers to be shown.
  - If you select **Symmetrical**, specify the **Upper value**.
  - For **Deviation** and **Limits**, specify the **Upper value** and **Lower value**.
  - If you want the tolerance values to appear smaller than the dimension text, specify **Scaling for height**.
  - Specify the **Vertical position** of the dimension text with regard to the tolerance values (**Bottom**, **Middle**, or **Top**).
- If **Deviation** or **Limits** is selected, choose whether to **Align decimal separators** or **Align operational symbols**. See the following illustration:

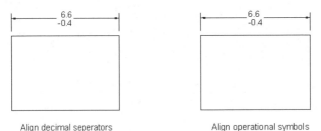

Align decimal seperators   Align operational symbols

- If you are showing **Alternate units**, specify the **Precision** of the numbers under the **Alternate units tolerance**.
- Specify the **Zero suppression** for both the **Primary units** tolerance and the **Alternate units** tolerance.

9.11 CREATING A SUB STYLE

- Sometimes you need a dimension style identical to almost all types of dimensions except for **Diameter**, for example.
- In this case, we create a dimension style for all types, and then we create a sub dimension style from it.
- Perform the following steps:
  - Create your dimension style.
  - Select it from the list in the **Dimension Style** dialog box.
  - Click the **New** button to create a new style.
  - The following dialog box will appear:

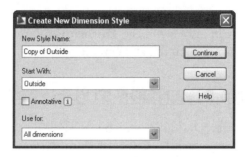

- For **Use for**, select **Diameter dimensions** (for example). The dialog box will change to:

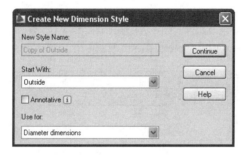

- Now, click **Continue** and make the changes you want. These changes only will affect the diameter dimensions.
- In the **Dimension Style** dialog box, you will see something like the following:

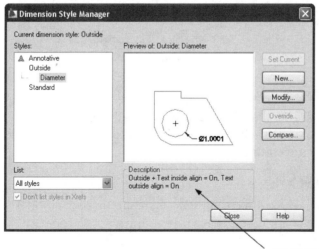

The differences between the
dimension style and the sub-style

- You can see how AutoCAD relates the new sub style to the existing style. You can also see in the **Description** area how AutoCAD lists the differences between the style and its sub style.

9.12 CONTROLLING DIMENSION STYLES

- Once you have created more than one dimension style, you can control these dimension styles using the **Current**, **Modify**, and **Delete** buttons.

Set Dimension Style Current

- While you are in the **Dimension style** dialog box, select the desired dimension style and click the **Current** button.
- Make sure you are in the **Annotate** tab on the **Ribbon**, and, using the **Dimensions** panel, select the current dimension style from the pop-up list:

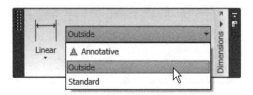

- Make sure you are in the **Home** tab on the **Ribbon**, and, expanding the **Annotation** panel, use the pop-up list to set the current dimension style:

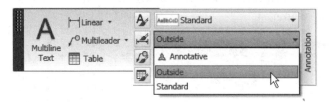

Modify Dimension Style

- While you are in the **Dimension Style** dialog box, select the desired dimension style and click the **Modify** button. The same dialog box will appear for more editing.

Delete Dimension Style

- In order to delete a dimension style there are three conditions:
  - It should be not used in the current drawing.
  - It should not be the current dimension style.
  - It should not have any sub style. If it does, delete the sub style (child) first and then delete the main style (parent).

- If these three conditions are fulfilled, select the desired dimension style to be deleted and press [Del] (you can also select it and right-click, and then select **Delete**). The following dialog box will appear:

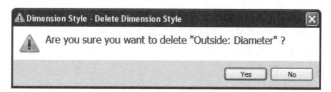

- If you click **Yes**, it will be deleted. If you click **No**, the whole process will be canceled.

CREATING DIMENSION STYLES (METRIC)

Workshop 17-A

1. Start AutoCAD 2010.
2. Open the file *Workshop_17.dwg*.
3. Create a new dimension style and name it **Outside**, starting from **Standard**, and use for **All dimensions**. (Anything not mentioned here should be left at the default value or setting.)
4. Under **Line** make the following changes:
   a. **Extend beyond dim line** = 0.25
   b. **Offset from origin** = 0.15
5. Under **Symbols and Arrows** make the following changes:
   a. **Arrowhead, First** = Oblique
   b. **Arrow size** = 0.25
6. Under **Text** make the following changes:
   a. **Text style** = Dimension
   b. **Text placement, Vertical** = Above
   c. **Text alignment** = Aligned with dimension line
7. Under **Fit** make the following changes:
   a. **Use overall scale** = 1000
8. Under **Primary Units** make the following changes:
   a. **Linear dimension, Precision** = 0.00
   b. **Suffix** = m
   c. **Scale Factor** = 0.001
9. Create a new style and name it **Inside**, starting from **Outside**, and use for **All dimensions**.

10. Under **Lines** make the following changes:

    a. **Extension lines, Suppress Ext line 1** = on, **Ext line 2** = on

11. Under **Symbols and Arrows** make the following changes:

    a. **Arrow size** = 0.20

12. Under **Text** make the following changes:

    a. **Text style** = Standard

    b. **Text height** = 0.25

13. Under **Fit** make the following changes:

    a. **Fine tuning, Place text manually** = on

14. Make a sub style from **Outside** for **Radius dimensions**.

15. Under **Symbols and Arrows** make the following changes:

    a. **Arrowheads, Second** = Closed filled

16. Under **Text** make the following changes:

    a. **Text alignment** = ISO Standard

17. Save the file and close it.

CREATING DIMENSION STYLES (IMPERIAL)

Workshop 17-B

1. Start AutoCAD 2010.

2. Open the file *Workshop_17.dwg*.

3. Create a new dimension style and name it **Outside**, starting from **Standard**, and use for **All dimensions**. (Anything not mentioned here should be left at the default value or setting.)

4. Under **Line** make the following changes:

    a. **Extend beyond dim line** = 3/4"

    b. **Offset from origin** = 1/2"

5. Under **Symbols and Arrows** make the following changes:

    a. **Arrowhead, First** = Oblique

    b. **Arrow size** = 3/4"

6. Under **Text** make the following changes:

    a. **Text style** = Dimension

    b. **Text placement, Vertical** = Above

    c. **Text alignment** = Aligned with dimension line

7. Under **Fit** make the following changes:
   a. **Use overall scale** = 12
8. Under **Primary Units** make the following changes:
   a. **Unit Format** = Architectural, **Precision** = 0'-0"
   b. **Suffix** = ft
9. Create a new style and name it **Inside**, starting from **Outside**, and use for **All dimensions**.
10. Under **Lines** make the following changes:
    a. **Extension lines, Suppress Ext line 1** = on, **Ext line 2** = on
11. Under **Text** make the following changes:
    a. **Text style** = Standard (change the font to be Arial)
    b. **Text height** = 3/4"
12. Under **Fit** make the following changes:
    a. **Fine tuning, Place text manually** = on
13. Make a sub style from **Outside** for **Radius dimensions**.
14. Under **Symbols and Arrows** make the following changes:
    a. **Arrowheads, Second** = Closed filled
15. Under **Text** make the following changes:
    a. **Text alignment** = ISO Standard.
16. Save the file and close it.

9.13 AN INTRODUCTION TO DIMENSIONING COMMANDS

- Dimensioning commands insert dimensions using the points specified by a user.
- You will find all commands under the **Annotate** tab in the **Dimensions** panel:

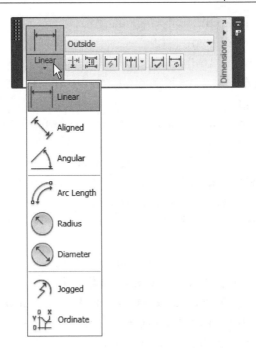

- More commands can be found in the hidden part of the **Dimensions** panel:

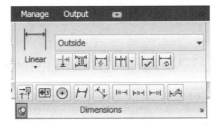

- For the purpose of this book, all dimensioning commands will be found in the **Dimensions** panel.

9.14 THE LINEAR COMMAND

- Use the **Linear** command to create a horizontal or vertical dimension.
- To start the **Linear** command, make sure you are in the **Annotate** tab on the **Ribbon**, and, using the **Dimensions** panel, click the **Linear** button.
- The following prompt will appear:

```
Specify first extension line origin or <select object>:
```
(Specify the first point)
```
Specify second extension line origin:
```
(Specify the second point)
```
Specify dimension line location or
[Mtext/Text/Angle/Horizontal/Vertical/Rotated]:
```
(Specify the location of the dimension line)

- There are three steps to follow:
  - Specify the first point of the dimension distance to be measured.
  - Specify the second point of the dimension distance to be measured.
  - Specify the location of the dimension block by specifying the location of the dimension line.
- The following is the result:

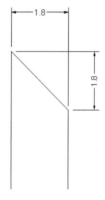

- You can use the other options available. They are:
  - **Mtext**
  - **Text**
  - **Angle**
  - **Horizontal**
  - **Vertical**
  - **Rotated**

Mtext

- To edit the measured distance in the **MTEXT** command.

Text

- To edit the measured distance in the **DTEXT** command.

Angle

- To change the angle of the text.

Horizontal

- To create a horizontal dimension.

Vertical

- To create a vertical dimension.

Rotated

- To create a dimension line parallel to another angle given by the user. As in the case of projecting a distance over another angle. See the following illustration:

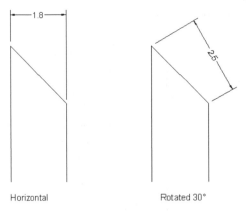

Horizontal   Rotated 30°

9.15 THE ALIGNED COMMAND

- The **Aligned** command is used to create a dimension parallel to the measured distance.
- To start the **Aligned** command, make sure you are in the **Annotate** tab on the **Ribbon**, and, using the **Dimensions** panel, click the **Aligned** button.
- The following prompt will appear:

```
Specify first extension line origin or <select object>:
(Specify the first point)
Specify second extension line origin: (Specify the
second point)
Specify dimension line location or
[Mtext/Text/Angle]: (Specify the location of the
dimension line)
```

- There are three steps to follow:
  - Specify the first point of the dimension distance to be measured.

- Specify the second point of the dimension distance to be measured.
- Specify the location of the dimension block by specifying the location of the dimension line.

■ The following is the result:

■ The rest of the options are the same as the **Linear** command.

LINEAR AND ALIGNED DIMENSIONS

Exercise 34
1. Start AutoCAD 2010.
2. Open the file *Exercise_34.dwg*.
3. Make the **Dimension** layer current.
4. Make the linear and aligned dimensions as shown:

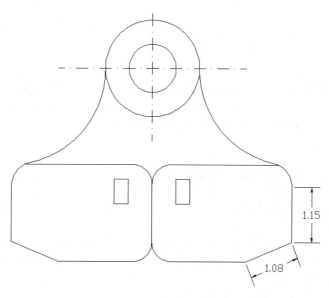

5. Save the file and close it.

9.16 THE ANGULAR COMMAND

- The **Angular** command is used to create an angular dimension.
- To start the **Angular** command, make sure you are in the **Annotate** tab on the **Ribbon**, and, using the **Dimensions** panel, click the **Angular** button.
- There are four ways to place an angular dimension in AutoCAD:
  - Select an arc and AutoCAD will measure the included angle.
  - Select a circle. The position that you select the circle from will be the first point and the center of the circle will be the second point. AutoCAD will ask the user to specify any point on the diameter of the circle and will place the angle accordingly.
  - Select two lines. AutoCAD will measure either the inside angle or the outside angle.
  - Select a vertex, which will be considered a center point, then AutoCAD will ask you to specify two points and will measure either the inside angle or the outside angle.

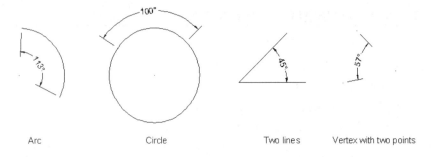

Arc   Circle   Two lines   Vertex with two points

- The following prompts will appear:

```
Select arc, circle, line, or <specify vertex>: (Select the
desired method as discussed above—assume we select arc)
Specify dimension arc line location or [Mtext/Text/Angle]:
(Specify the dimension block location)
```

9.17 THE ARC LENGTH COMMAND

- The **Arc Length** command is used to create a dimension showing the length of the selected arc.
- To start the **Arc Length** command, make sure you are in the **Annotate** tab on the **Ribbon**, and, using the **Dimensions** panel, click the **Arc Length** button.
- The following prompt will appear:

```
Select arc or polyline arc segment: (Select the desired arc)
Specify arc length dimension location, or [Mtext/Text/Angle/
Partial/Leader]: (Specify the location of the dimension block)
```

- There are two steps to follow:
  - Select the desired arc.
  - Specify the location of the dimension block.
- The following is the result:

- The options **Mtext**, **Text**, and **Angle**—which are available to the **Arc Length** command—were discussed in the **Linear** command section.

Partial

- If you want **Arc Length** to measure part of the arc and not the entire arc, specify the two points on the arc. The result looks something like this:

Leader

- To add a leader, see the following example:

9.18 THE RADIUS COMMAND

- The **Radius** command is used to put a radius dimension on an arc and/or a circle.
- To start the **Radius** command, make sure you are in the **Annotate** tab on the **Ribbon**, and, using the **Dimensions** panel, click the **Radius** button.

- The following prompts will appear:

```
Select arc or circle: (Select the desired arc or circle)
Specify dimension line location, or
[Mtext/Text/Angle]: (Specify the location of the dimension
block)
```

- There are two steps to follow:
  - Select the desired arc or circle.
  - Specify the location of the dimension block.
- As a result, you will see:

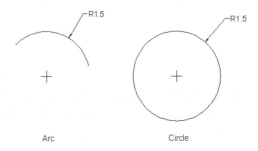

Arc   Circle

9.19 THE DIAMETER COMMAND

- The **Diameter** command is used to put diameter dimensions on an arc and/or a circle.
- To start the **Diameter** command, make sure you are in the **Annotate** tab on the **Ribbon**, and, using the **Dimensions** panel, click the **Diameter** button.
- The following prompts will appear:

```
Select arc or circle: (Select the desired arc or
circle)Specify dimension line location, or
[Mtext/Text/Angle]: (Specify the dimension block
location)
```

- As a result, you will see the following:

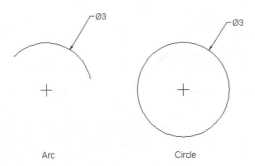

Arc   Circle

9.20 THE JOGGED COMMAND

- If you have a large arc, then its center is very far from the arc itself. Therefore, it is difficult for users to add a normal radius dimension.
- The solution is to add a jogged radius dimension.
- The **Jogged** command is used to add a jogged radius to an arc or a circle.
- To start the **Jogged** command, make sure you are in the **Annotate** tab on the **Ribbon**, and, using the **Dimensions** panel, click the **Jogged** button.
- The following prompts will appear:

```
Select arc or circle: (Select the desired arc or
circle)Specify center location override: (Specify a point
which will act as a new center point)
Dimension text = 1.5
Specify dimension line location or
[Mtext/Text/Angle]: (Specify the dimension line location)
Specify jog location: (Specify the location of the jog)
```

- There are four steps to follow:
  - Select the desired arc or circle.
  - Specify the point that will act as the new center point.
  - Specify the dimension line location.
  - Specify the location of the jog.
- Once you complete the four steps, you will see:

9.21 THE ORDINATE COMMAND

- The **Ordinate** command is used to add several measurements to objects relative to a certain point.
- To start the **Ordinate** command, make sure you are in the **Annotate** tab on the **Ribbon**, and, using the **Dimensions** panel, click the **Ordinate** button.
- The **Ordinate** command allows you to set dimensions relative to a datum, either in X or in Y. See the following illustration:

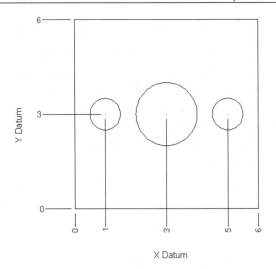

- You have to change the UCS (User Coordinate System) origin location to the desired location, otherwise, the values will be relative to the current location of 0,0.
- The following prompts will appear:

```
Specify feature location: (Click on the desired point)
Specify leader endpoint or
[Xdatum/Ydatum/Mtext/Text/Angle]: (Specify the dimension
location)
```

- By default, when you select a point, you may go in the direction of X or Y. If you want the **Ordinate** command to go exclusively in the X direction, then select the **Xdatum** option, or select **Ydatum** if you want to go exclusively in the Y direction.
- The additional options are the same as those in the **Linear** command.

ANGULAR, ARC LENGTH, RADIUS, DIAMETER, AND DIMENSIONS

Exercise 35
1. Start AutoCAD 2010.
2. Open the file *Exercise_35.dwg*.
3. Make the following modification to the current dimension style (i.e., **Standard**):
   a. Under **Text**, change the current text style to use **Arial** font.
4. Perform the steps for the five types of dimensions as shown:

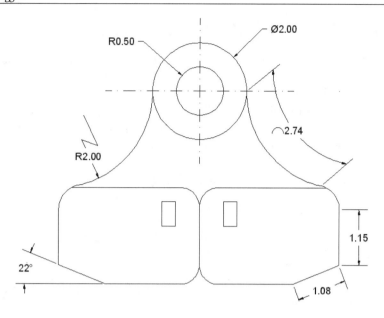

5. Save the file and close it.

ORDINATE AND JOGGED

Exercise 36
1. Start AutoCAD 2010.
2. Open the file *Exercise_36.dwg*.
3. Create the ordinate and jogged dimensions as shown:

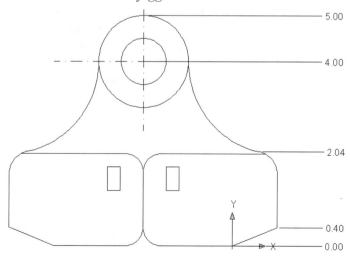

4. Save the file and close it.

9.22 THE CONTINUE COMMAND

- After you put a dimension in your drawing (i.e., linear, aligned, angular, or ordinate), you can ask AutoCAD to continue using the same type and allocate it along the first one.
- The **Continue** command will allow you to input many dimensions swiftly.
- To start the **Continue** command, make sure you are in the **Annotate** tab on the **Ribbon**, and, using the **Dimensions** panel, click the **Continue** button.

If No Dimension Was Created in This Session

- The following prompt will appear:

```
Select continued dimension: (Select either Linear,
Aligned, Ordinate, or Angular)
```

- AutoCAD will consider the selected dimension as the base dimension and will continue accordingly.

If a Dimension Was Created in This Session

- The following prompt will appear:

```
Specify a second extension line origin or [Undo/Select]
<Select>: (Specify the second point of the last Linear,
Aligned, Ordinate, or Angular, or select an existing
dimension)
```

- AutoCAD will give you the ability to do one of three things:
  - If you already input a linear dimension (for example), then you can continue by specifying the second point, considering the second point of the first dimension is the first point of the continuing dimension.
  - You can select an existing dimension and continue from there.
  - You can undo the last continue dimension.
- See the following illustration:

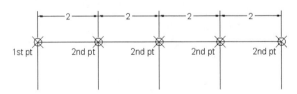

9.23 THE BASELINE COMMAND

- The **Baseline** command works just like the **Continue** command except the dimensions will always be related to the first point the user selected.
- To start the **Baseline** command, make sure you are in the **Annotate** tab on the **Ribbon**, and, using the **Dimensions** panel, click the **Baseline** button.
- All of the prompts and procedures are identical to the **Continue** command.
- See the following illustration:

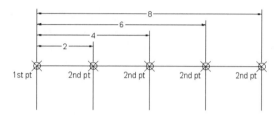

CONTINUOUS AND BASELINE DIMENSIONS

Exercise 37

1. Start AutoCAD 2010.
2. Open the file *Exercise_37.dwg*.
3. Create the continuous and baseline dimensions as shown:

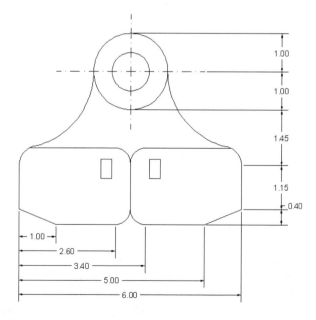

4. Save the file and close it.

9.24 THE QUICK DIMENSION COMMAND

- The **Quick Dimension** command is used to place a group of dimensions in a single step.
- To start the **Quick Dimension** command, make sure you are in the **Annotate** tab on the **Ribbon**, and, using the **Dimensions** panel, click the **Quick Dimension** button.
- The following prompt will appear:

```
Select geometry to dimension: (Either by clicking, Window,
or Crossing, after you are done press [Enter])
Specify dimension line position, or
[Continuous/Staggered/Baseline/Ordinate/Radius/
Diameter/datumPoint/Edit/seTtings] <Continuous>:
```

- At this prompt you can right-click and the following shortcut menu will appear:

- From this shortcut menu, you can select the proper dimension type. You can choose from: **Continuous**, **Staggered**, **Baseline**, **Ordinate**, **Radius**, or **Diameter**.
- Select the type and then specify the dimension line location; a group of dimensions will be placed in a single step.

- See the following **Staggered** example:

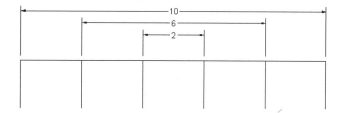

9.25 DIMENSION BLOCKS AND GRIPS

- You can edit dimension blocks using **Grips**.
- If you click a dimension block, five grips will appear, just like the following:

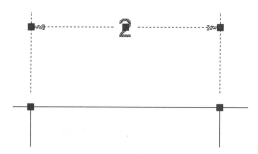

- As you can see, the grips appear in the following places:
  - The two ends of the dimension line.
  - The two origins of the dimension line.
  - The dimension text.
- You can change the position of the text by clicking its grip and moving it parallel to the dimension line.
- You can change the position of the dimension line by clicking one of the two grips and moving it closer to, or farther from, the origin.
- You can change the measured distance by moving one of the two grips of the origin, so the distance will change accordingly.
- See the following example:

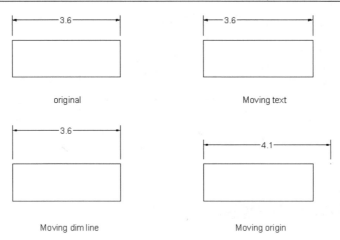

original   Moving text

Moving dim line   Moving origin

- Also, if you select a dimension block and right-click, the following shortcut menu will appear (only the part concerning the dimension is shown):

- You can change **Dim Text Position**, **Precision**, **Dim Style**, and **Flip Arrow** in the selected dimension block.

Dim Text Position

- You can change the position of the dimension text as seen in the example.

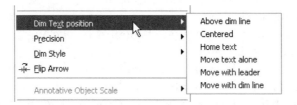

- **Above dim line**: The dimension text will move from any other position to **Above**.
- **Centered**: The dimension text will move from any other position to **Centered**.
- **Home text**: The dimension text will be restored to its original position according to its dimension style.

- **Move text alone**: Allows you to position the text freely.
- **Move with leader**: Allows you to position the text freely, but with a leader.
- **Move with dim line**: Allows you to move both the dimension text and the dimension line in one single step.

Precision

- This will allow users to set the number of decimal places for the number shown.
- You can start from zero decimal places up to eight decimal places.

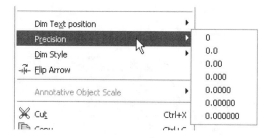

Dim Style

- The changes made using this method can be saved in a new dimension style using the **Save as New Style** option. Type in a new name.
- You can change the dimension style of any dimension block in the drawing. The existing dimension styles will appear in a pop-up menu; select the new desired dimension style.

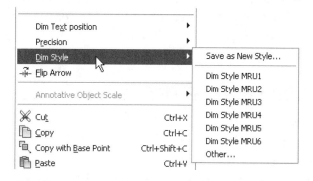

Flip Arrow

- This method is used to flip the arrows from inside to outside, and vice versa.
- The process can be done on only one arrow at a time.

9.26 DIMENSION BLOCK PROPERTIES

- Select a dimension block and right-click, and then select **Properties**. The following dialog box will appear:

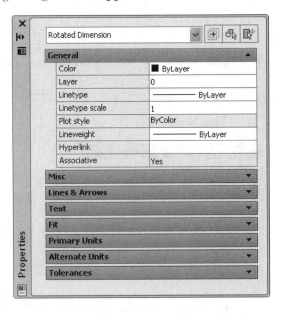

- Under **General**, you will see the general properties of the selected dimension block.
- You will see the following properties: **Misc**, **Lines & Arrows**, **Text**, **Fit**, **Primary Units**, **Alternate Units**, and **Tolerances**. If you compare these to the **Dimension Style** command, you will find them identical, which means you can change any of the characteristics of the dimension block after it goes through **Properties**.

QUICK DIMENSION AND EDITING

Exercise 38

1. Start AutoCAD 2010.
2. Open the file *Exercise_38.dwg*.
3. Using the **Quick Dimension** command and **Crossing**, select all of the lines and the two arcs at the bottom of the shape.
4. Deselect the two arcs along with the middle vertical line and press [Enter], then right-click and select the baseline, and put it in a convenient place beneath the shape.

5. Select the dimension with **value** = 1.00 (the left-most spot). Five grips will appear.
6. Make sure that **Middle** in **OSNAP** is turned on. Select the upper right-hand grip to make it hot and move it to the middle point of the right horizontal line.
7. The value of the dimension should read 1.80. Press [Esc] twice.
8. Select the same dimension block again and move the dimension line closer to the shape. Press [Esc] twice.
9. Select the lower dimension with **value** = 6.00.
10. Right-click and change the **Precision** of the number to 0.0000 and make it **Above dim line**.
11. Select the dimension with **value** = 5.00 and show the **Properties** palette.
12. Change **Arrow 1** and **Arrow 2** to be **Oblique**, and the **arrow size** = 0.3.
13. The shape should look like the following:

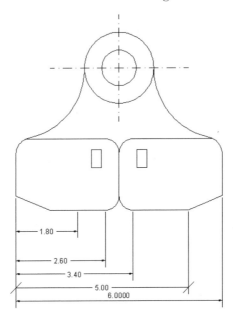

14. Save the file and close it.

9.27 AN INTRODUCTION TO THE MULTILEADER

- A leader in AutoCAD is an arrow pointing to a part of the drawing, with two lines and some text to explain certain facts about that part.
- A multileader can be one arrow with a single set of lines or multiple arrows with multiple sets of lines. See the following illustration of a single leader:

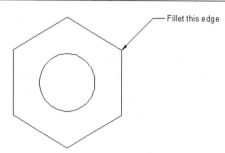

- See the following illustration of a multileader:

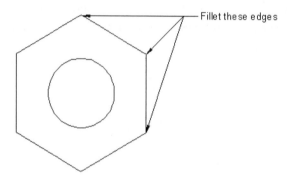

 - Normally, you will create a single leader and you can create a multileader from it using other commands.
- You will specify (by default) two points; the first one is where the arrow will be pointing to and the second one will specify the length and angle of the leader. Another small horizontal landing will be added automatically. See the following illustration:

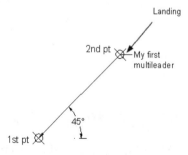

- A multileader has its own style and set of commands, which we will discuss in the coming pages.

9.28 MULTILEADER: CREATING THE STYLE

- As we discussed in **Dimension Style**, you will use **Multileader Style** to set the characteristics of the multileader block.
- To start the **Multileader Style** command, make sure you are in the **Annotate** tab on the **Ribbon**, and, using the **Leaders** panel, click the **Multileader Style** button.

- The following dialog box will appear:

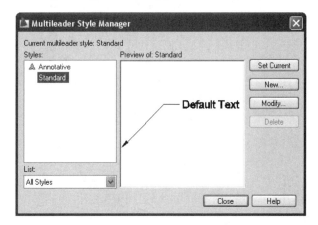

- To create a new style, click the **New** button. The following dialog box will appear:

- Type the name of the new style and select the existing style that you want to start with. Click **Continue** to start modifying the **Multileader style**.

- You will see three tabs:
  - **Leader Format**
  - **Leader Structure**
  - **Content**
- We will discuss each one of these in the coming pages.

Leader Format

- You will see the following dialog box:

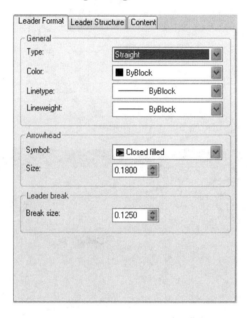

- You have three choices for the type of leader:
  - **Straight**
  - **Spline**
  - **None**
- See the following illustration:

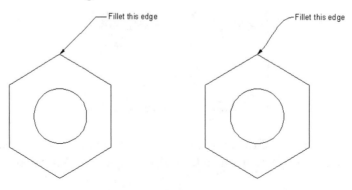

- You can choose the **Color**, **Linetype**, and **Lineweight** in the same way as the **Dimension Style** command.
- Choose the **Arrowhead Symbol** (from 20 different existing shapes) and its size.
- If there is **Dimension Break**, how large will the break of the multileader be? Answer this question by setting the **Break size** value.

Leader Structure

- You will see the following dialog box:

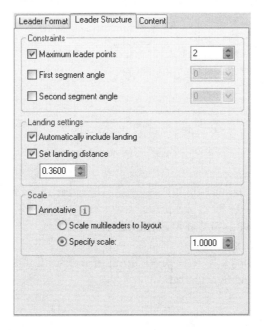

- Specify the **Maximum leader points**. As discussed earlier, the default value is 2, and you can specify more points.
- By default, you will specify the **First segment angle** and a small horizontal landing (**Second segment angle**) will be added, but you can set the angle values for both in the **Multileader style**.
- Choose whether to **Automatically include landing** or not. If you select to include it, you must determine the **landing length**.
- Select whether the multileader will be **Annotative** or not. (We will leave it off for now.)

Content

- You will see the following dialog box:

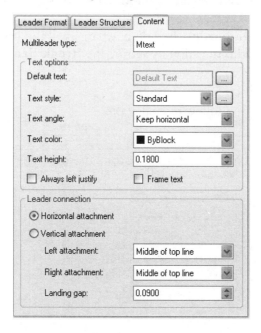

- There are two types of **Multileader**:
  - With **Mtext**
  - With a **Block** (either predefined or user-defined)
- See the following illustration:

- **Mtext** (Multiline text) is selected by default. To adjust the settings:
  - If there is any text that should appear each time, type it in **Default text**.
  - Specify the **Text style**.
  - Specify the **Text angle** (**Keep horizontal**, **Right-reading**, or **As inserted**).
  - Specify the **Text Color** and **Text height** (if **Text Style** height = 0).
  - Specify whether to make the text **Always left justify** or not, and with **Frame** or not.
  - Control the position of the text relative to the landing for both left and right leader lines.
  - Control the gap distance between the end of the landing and the text.

- If you select the **Multileader type** to be **Block**, you will see the following dialog box:

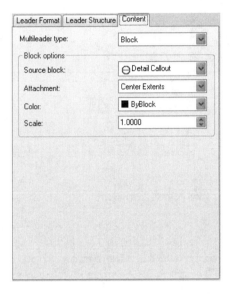

- Adjust the following settings:
  - Specify the **Source block** (choose from the list) or select **User Block**. The following dialog box will appear:

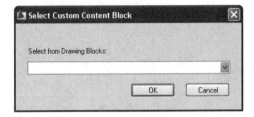

  - Type the name of the desired block and click **OK**.
  - Specify the **Attachment** position.
  - Specify the **Color** of the attachment.
  - Specify the **Scale** of the attachment.

9.29 MULTILEADER COMMANDS

- After you finish creating **Multileader Style**, you are now ready to insert the multileader into your drawing.
- You will always start with the **Multileader** command to insert a single leader.

- To start the **Multileader** command, make sure you are in the **Annotate** tab on the **Ribbon**, and, using the **Leaders** panel, click the **Multileader** button.

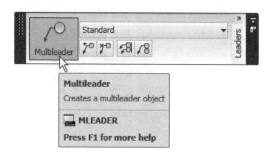

- The following prompts will appear:

```
Specify leader arrowhead location or [leader Landing first/
Content first/Options] <Options>:
(Specify the point which the arrow should point to)
Specify leader landing location: (Specify the angle and the
length of the leader)
```

- Type in the text you want to appear in the leader.
- Click the **Add Leader** button to add more leaders (arrows) to an existing single leader:

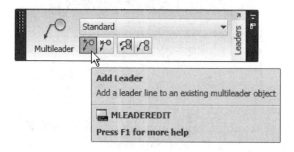

- The following prompts will appear:

```
Select a multileader:
1 found
Specify leader arrowhead location:
Specify leader arrowhead location:
```

- Click the **Remove Leader** button to remove some leaders from an existing multileader.

- The following prompts will appear:

```
Select a multileader:
1 found
Specify leaders to remove:
Specify leaders to remove:
```

- Click the **Align** button to arrange several multileaders in the same line.

- The following prompts will appear:

```
Select multileaders: 1 found
Select multileaders: 1 found, 2 total
Select multileaders: (Press [Enter])
Current mode: Use current spacing
Select multileader to align to or [Options]:
Specify direction:
```

- Click the **Collect** button to collect several multileaders into a single leader. This command only works with leaders containing blocks:

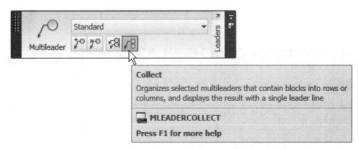

■ You will see the following prompts:

```
Select multileaders:
Select multileaders: (Press [Enter] when you are done)
Specify collected multileader location or [Vertical/
Horizontal/Wrap] <Horizontal>:
```

MULTILEADER

Exercise 39

1. Start AutoCAD 2010.
2. Open the file *Exercise_39.dwg*.
3. Using **Material style** and **Free-Block style**, add the following multileader:

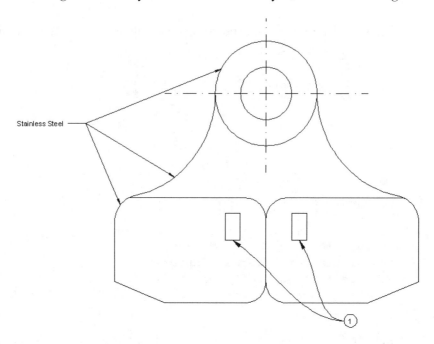

4. Save the file and close it.

PUTTING DIMENSIONS ON THE PLAN (METRIC)

Workshop 18-A

1. Start AutoCAD 2010.
2. Open the file *Workshop_18.dwg*.

3. Make the **Dimension** layer the current layer.

4. Freeze the following layers: **Furniture**, **Hatch**, and **Text**.

5. Using **Outside** and **Inside** dimension styles, add the dimensions for the outer and inner dimensions as shown:

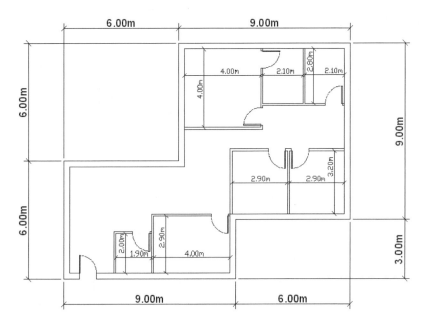

6. Save the file and close it.

PUTTING DIMENSIONS ON THE PLAN (IMPERIAL)

 Workshop 18-B

1. Start AutoCAD 2010.

2. Open the file *Workshop_18.dwg*.

3. Make the **Dimension** layer the current layer.

4. Freeze the following layers: **Furniture, Hatch**, and **Text**.

5. Using **Outside** and **Inside** dimension styles, add the dimensions for the outer and inner dimensions as shown:

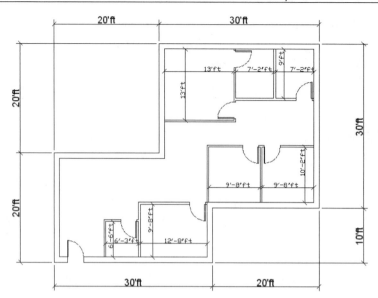

6. Save the file and close it.

CHAPTER REVIEW

1. You can only create dimension styles that will affect all dimension types.
   a. True
   b. False

2. _____ and _____ are two types of dimensions that you can use with arcs.

3. Which one of the following is not an AutoCAD dimension command?
   a. **dimlinear**
   b. **dimarc**
   c. **dimchordlength**
   d. **dimaligned**

4. The only way to add an **Angular dimension** is to have two lines.
   a. True
   b. False

5. Which of the following is a type of **Tolerance** in AutoCAD?
   a. **Deviation**
   b. **Symmetrical**
   c. **Limits**
   d. All of the above

6. In order to make a dimension style _____, double-click the name in the **Dimension Style** dialog box.

CHAPTER REVIEW ANSWERS

1. b
2. **Arc length, Jogged, Radius, Diameter**
3. c
4. b
5. d
6. current

Chapter 10

Plotting Your Drawing

In This Chapter

- ◊ Introduction
- ◊ **Model Space** Versus **Paper Space**
- ◊ Introduction to **Layouts**
- ◊ How to Switch between **Model Space** and **Layouts**
- ◊ How to Create a New Layout
- ◊ What Is the **Page Setup Manager**?
- ◊ **Layouts** and **Viewports**
- ◊ Adding **Viewports** to **Layouts**
- ◊ **Model Space** and **Paper Space** Modes in **Layouts**
- ◊ Modifying, Scaling, and Maximizing **Viewports**
- ◊ Freezing Layers in **Viewports**
- ◊ Layer Override in **Viewports**
- ◊ An Introduction to **Plot Style Tables**
- ◊ The **Color-Dependent Plot Style Table**
- ◊ The **Named Plot Style Table**
- ◊ The **Plot** Command
- ◊ What Is a DWF File?
- ◊ What Is a DWFx File?
- ◊ Exporting DWF, DWFx, and PDF Files
- ◊ The **Publish** Command
- ◊ How to View DWF and DWFx Files

10.1 INTRODUCTION

- Before AutoCAD® 2000, almost all AutoCAD users plotted from **Model Space**, which is where they created their design.
- In AutoCAD 2000, the development of **Layouts** made it easy for everyone to shift their attention to the new method, which encompassed many new features and surpassed plotting from **Model Space**.

- Also, in AutoCAD 2000, a new feature was introduced called **Plot Style**, which allowed users to create color-independent configuration plotting.
- Eventhough AutoCAD 2000 was a flagship version in more ways than one, the most important features were the new improvements in the plotting process.

10.2 MODEL SPACE VERSUS PAPER SPACE

- **Model Space** is where you create the drawing using all of the modification processes.
- When you think about plotting, you should use **Paper Space**.
- There is only one **Model Space** in each drawing file.
- Before AutoCAD 2000, there was only one **Paper Space** per drawing file.
- Beginning with AutoCAD 2000, **Paper Space** was changed to **Layout**.
- You can create as many layouts as you wish in each drawing file.
- Each **Layout** will be connected to **Page Setup**, where you will specify at least three things. They are:
  - The plotter to be used.
  - The paper size to be used.
  - The paper orientation (portrait or landscape).
- To demonstrate the importance of this feature, let's take a look at the following example: we have a company who owns an A0 plotter, an A2 printer, and an A4 laser printer. The staff will use all of these printers to print a single drawing.
  - If you use **Model Space**, you will change the setup of the printer, paper size, and paper orientation, along with the drawing area to be plotted each and every time you want to print.
  - But if you create three layouts with the proper **Page Setup**, printing will be fast and easy; simply go to the layout and issue the **Plot** command, which will save time, effort, and money!

10.3 AN INTRODUCTION TO LAYOUTS

- Each layout consists of the **Page Setup**, **Objects**, and **Viewports**.
  - **Page Setup**: Is where you will specify the printer (or plotter), the paper size, and the paper orientation, in addition to other items that will be covered later in this chapter.
  - **Objects**: These include blocks (e.g., the title block), text, dimensions, and any other desired objects.
  - **Viewports**: Viewports will be covered later in this chapter.

- See the following illustration:

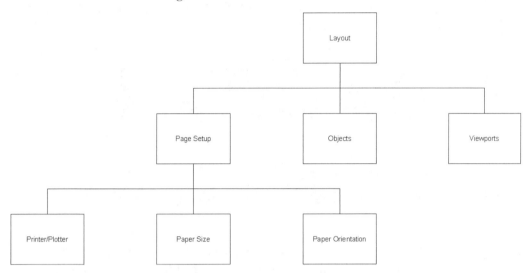

- Each layout should have a name. AutoCAD will give it a temporary name, but you can change it.
- By default, when you create a new drawing using the *acad.dwt* template, two layouts—**Layout1** and **Layout2**—will be created automatically.
- You can choose to have the **Page Setup Manager** dialog box appear when you click on a layout for the first time, for the purpose of setting the printer, paper size, etc.
- **Layouts** and **Page Setup** will be saved in the drawing file.
- By default, **Page Setup** has no name, but you can name it accordingly, use it in other layouts in the current drawing file, or in other drawings.

10.4 HOW TO SWITCH BETWEEN MODEL SPACE AND LAYOUTS

- By default, AutoCAD will be in **Model Space** when you begin a new drawing.
- On the **Status Bar** you will find the following:

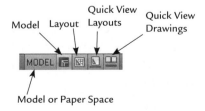

- Before you click on the **Layout** button, it is preferable to click the **Quick View Layouts** button to see the available layouts saved in your drawing. See the following illustration:

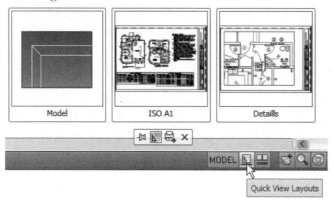

- In this illustration, you can see two layouts. You can choose which to view by clicking on the small view. Also, you can **Publish**, create a **New Layout**, or choose to **Pin Quick View Layouts**.
- In order to jump from **Model Space** to **Layout** and vice versa, click on the **Model Space** and **Layout** buttons in the **Status Bar**.
- You can also right-click either **Model Space** or **Layout** and the following shortcut menu will appear:

Display Layout and Model Tabs

- If you select the **Display Layout and Model Tabs**, you will see the following tabs in the lower left-hand corner of the **Graphical Area**:

Model   ISO A1   Details

- This information is essential to what we will discuss in the next section.

10.5 HOW TO CREATE A NEW LAYOUT

- There are several ways to create a new layout. You can select the **New Layout** option, use a template, or use the **Move or Copy** option.

New Layout

- **New Layout** is a very simple method. First, right-click on any existing layout name and a shortcut menu will appear. Select the **New Layout** option.
- A new layout will be added with a temporary name. You can right-click and select the **Rename** option.

Using a Template

- You can import any layout defined inside a template and use it in your current drawing file.
- Right-click on any existing layout and a shortcut menu will appear. Select the **From template** option and the following dialog box will appear:

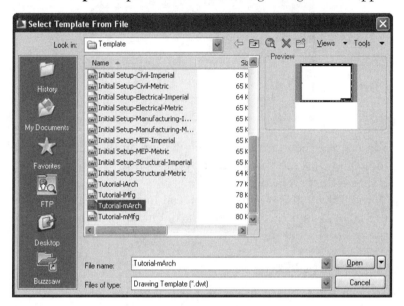

- Select the desired template and click **Open**. The following dialog box will appear:

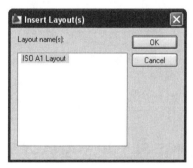

- Click on one of the listed layouts and click **OK**.

Move or Copy

- Using the **Move or Copy** option, you can move a layout to the left or right from its current position. Also, you can create a copy of an existing layout.

- Select the layout that you want to create a copy from and right-click. When the shortcut menu appears, select the **Move or Copy** option. The following dialog box will appear:

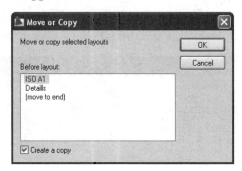

- You can see there are two existing layouts in the dialog box. Select one of them and click the **Create a copy** check box.
- Rename the new layout.

 - Without using this command, you can move the layout position relative to the other layouts by clicking the layout name, holding it, and dragging it to the position required.

Copying Using the Mouse

- You can also copy any layout by performing the following steps:
  - Click the name of the layout to be copied.
  - Hold the [Ctrl] key on the keyboard.
  - Hold and drag the mouse to the new position of the newly copied layout.

  - Rename the new layout.

10.6 WHAT IS THE PAGE SETUP MANAGER?

- As mentioned previously, each layout will have a **Page Setup** linked to it.
- The **Page Setup Manager** is the dialog box in which you will create, modify, delete, and import **Page setups** for layouts.

- The easiest way to issue this command is to select the desired layout, right-click, and then select **Page Setup Manager**.
- The following dialog box will appear:

- At the top, you will see the **Current layout** name, and at the bottom, you will see the **Selected page setup details**.
- A check box will allow you to **Display (Page Setup Manager) when creating a new layout**, which is highly recommended.
- To create a new **Page Setup**, click the **New** button. The following dialog box will appear:

- Type in the name of the new **Page Setup** and click **OK**. The following dialog box will appear:

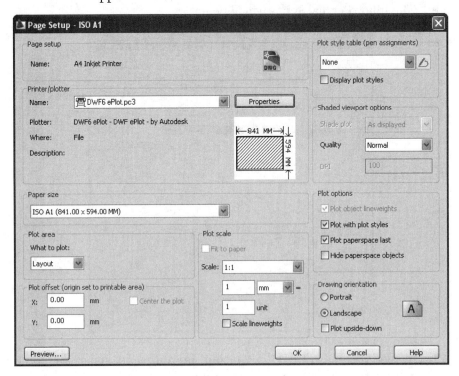

- Specify the **Name** of the printer or plotter you want to use (this printer should be installed and configured ahead of time).
- Specify the desired **Paper Size**.
- Specify **What to plot**. You have four choices: **Display**, **Extents**, **Layout**, and **Window**. If you are printing from **Model Space** (this is not recommended), then choose **Display**, **Extents**, or **Window**. If you will print from **Layout** (which is recommended), leave **Layout** as the default setting.
- Specify the **Plot Offset**. If you are using **Layout**, **Center the plot** will be off. **Center the plot** will be on if you are using other options, such as **Model Space**.
- Specify the **Plot Scale**. If you want to plot from **Layout**, then you will use the **viewports** (which will be discussed shortly), and you will specify a **Plot scale** for each viewport. Accordingly, you will set this **Plot scale** to 1 = 1. Specify if you would like to **scale lineweights** or not.

- Specify the **Plot style table (pen assignments)**, which will be discussed later in this chapter. Specify whether to **Display** the effects of the plot style on the layout or not.
- If you are plotting a 3D drawing and you want to plot it as shaded or rendered, specify the **Quality** of the shading or rendering.
- Specify the **Plot options**. They are:
  - Plot the objects with their lineweight as specified for each object and layer. This will only be available if you specify **None** for the **Plot style** setting.
  - Let the **Plot Style** control the lineweight of the objects and layers.
  - By default, **Paper Space** objects will be printed first, and then the **Model Space** objects. You have the option to change the printing order.
  - You can show or hide the **Paper Space** objects.
- Specify the **Paper orientation**, either **Portrait** or **Landscape**. By default, the printer will start printing from top to bottom. Change the specifications if you would like to print from bottom to top.
- When you are done, click **OK**. The **Page Setup** you create will be available for all layouts in the current drawing file.
- To link any layout in your drawing file to a certain **Page Setup**, go to the desired layout and start the **Page Setup Manager**. Select the **Page Setup** from the list and click **Set Current**. (Also, you can double-click the name of the **Page Setup**.) Now the current layout is linked to the **Page Setup** you select.
- To modify the settings of an existing **Page Setup**, click **Modify**.
- To use a saved **Page Setup** from an existing file, click **Import**.

CREATING LAYOUTS AND PAGE SETUP (METRIC)

Workshop 19-A
1. Start AutoCAD 2010.
2. Open the file *Workshop_19.dwg*.
3. Make sure the current layer is **Viewports**.
4. Using the **Status Bar**, right-click the **Layout1** icon, and select **Display Layout and Model tabs**.
5. Right-click on the name of any existing layout and select **From template**.
6. Select the template file *Tutorial-mArch.dwt*.

7. Select the layout named **ISO A1 Layout**.

8. Go to **ISO A1 Layout** and delete the only viewport in the layout (select its frame and press the [Del] key).

9. Delete **Layout2**.

10. Go to **Layout1**, rename it **Final**, and right-click the name of the layout. Select the **Page Setup Manager**.

11. Create a new **Page Setup** and name it **Final**.

12. Change the following settings:

    a. **Printer** = DWF6 ePlot.pc3

    b. **Paper Size** = ISO A3 (420 × 297 MM)

    c. **Orientation** = Landscape

    d. **Plot scale** = 1:1

13. Make **Final** the current page setup.

14. Erase the existing viewport.

15. Make the **Frame** layer current and insert the file with the name *ISO A3 Landscape Title Block.dwg* using 0,0 as the insertion point.

16. Save the file and close it.

CREATING LAYOUTS AND PAGE SETUP (IMPERIAL)

Workshop 19-B

1. Start AutoCAD 2010.

2. Open the file *Workshop_19.dwg*.

3. Make sure the current layer is **Viewports**.

4. Using the **Status Bar**, right-click the **Layout1** icon, and select **Display Layout and Model tabs**.

5. Right-click on the name of any existing layout and select **From template**.

6. Select the template file *Tutorial-iArch.dwt*.

7. Select the layout name **D-Size Layout**.

8. Go to **D-Size Layout** and delete the only viewport in the layout (select its frame and press the [Del] key).

9. Delete **Layout2**.

10. Go to **Layout1**, rename it **Final**, and right-click the name of the layout. Select the **Page Setup Manager**.

11. Create a new **Page Setup** and call it **Final**.
12. Change the following settings:
    a. **Printer** = DWF6 ePlot.pc3
    b. **Paper Size** = ANSI B (17 × 11 Inches)
    c. **Orientation** = Landscape
    d. **Plot scale** = 1:1
13. Make **Final** the current page setup.
14. Erase the existing viewport.
15. Make the **Frame** layer current and insert the file with the name *ANSI B Landscape Title Block.dwg* using 0,0 as the insertion point.
16. Save the file and close it.

10.7 LAYOUTS AND VIEWPORTS

- After creating a new layout, creating a **Page Setup**, and linking a **Page Setup** to the layout, you will see the following image:

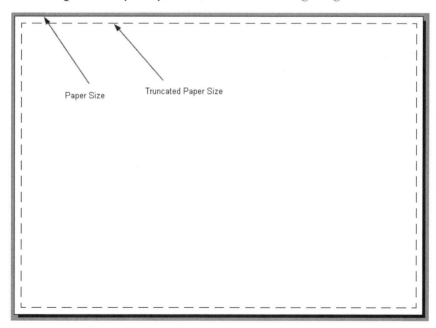

- The outer frame (solid) is the real paper size.

- The inner frame (dashed) is the truncated paper size, which is the paper size minus the printer margins.
  - Each printer comes from its manufacturer with built-in margins on all sides.
  - AutoCAD can read these margins from the printer driver accordingly.
  - Thus, you should read the printer manual in order to know exactly how wide the margins are on each side.
  - This will prove vital when you create the frame block of the establishment you will work in because you should create it within the truncated paper size rather than the full size.
- Printing from layouts is WYSIWYG (What You See Is What You Get).
- Also, by default, you will see that a single viewport of your drawing appears at the center of the paper size.
- As we said in the beginning of this chapter, we only have one **Model Space**, yet we can have as many **Layouts** as we wish. The **Viewport** is a rectangular shape (or any irregular shape) that contains a view of your **Model Space**.
- There are two types of **Viewports**: **Model Space** and **Layout**.
  - **Model Space Viewports**: These are always tiled, cannot be scaled, and the arrangement of viewports shown on the screen cannot be printed.
  - **Layout Viewports**: These can be tiled or separated, can be scaled, and the arrangement of viewports shown on the screen can be printed.
- See the following illustration:

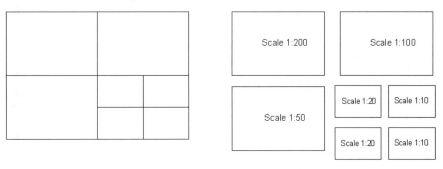

Model Space Viewports   Paper Space Viewports

10.8 ADDING VIEWPORTS TO LAYOUTS

- You can add viewports to layouts using several different methods:
  - Adding a single rectangular viewport or multiple rectangular viewports.

- Adding a single polygonal viewport.
- Converting an object to be a viewport.
- Clipping an existing viewport.
- We will discuss each method next.

Single or Multiple Rectangular Viewports

- You can add as many single or multiple rectangular viewports as you wish in any layout. You must specify two opposite corners in order to specify the area of the viewport(s).
- To start the **New Viewport** command, make sure you are in the **View** tab on the **Ribbon**, and, using the **Viewports** panel, click the **New** button.

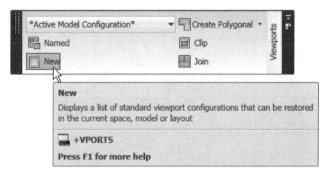

- The following dialog box will appear:

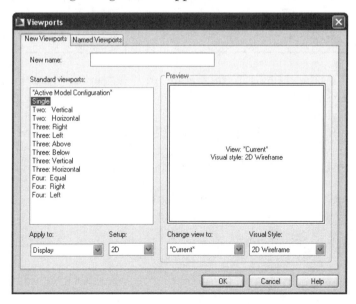

- From **Standard viewports**, select **Single** and then click **OK**. The following prompt will appear:

```
Specify first corner or [Fit] <Fit>:
Specify opposite corner:
```

- Just as we specify a window when we select objects, specify two opposite corners and a single viewport will be created.
- You will use the same dialog box:

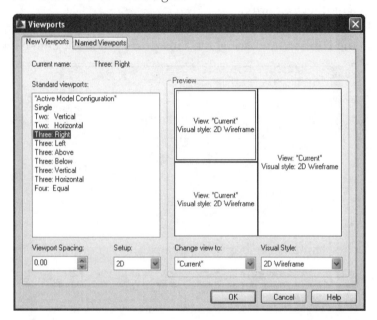

- Specify the desired arrangement. You can choose from **Two Horizontal** or **Two Vertical**, six different arrangements for three viewports, or one for four viewports.
- If you want the viewports to be tiled, leave the **Viewport Spacing** = 0. Otherwise, set a new value.
- Click **OK**. AutoCAD will display the following prompt:

```
Specify first corner or [Fit] <Fit>:
Specify opposite corner:
```

- See the following illustration:

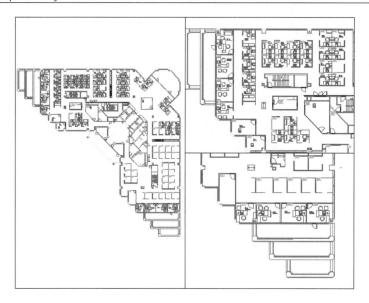

Single Polygonal Viewport

- The **Polygonal Viewport** command is used to add a single viewport with any irregular shape consisting of both straight lines and arcs.
- To start the **Polygonal Viewport** command, make sure you are in the **View** tab on the **Ribbon**, and, using the **Viewports** panel, click the **Polygonal** button.

- The following prompt will appear:

```
Specify corner of viewport or
[ON/OFF/Fit/Shadeplot/Lock/Object/Polygonal/
Restore/LAyer/2/3/4] <Fit>: _p
Specify start point:
```

```
Specify next point or [Arc/Length/Undo]:
Specify next point or [Arc/Close/Length/Undo]:
```

- It is almost identical to the **Pline** command.
- See the following illustration:

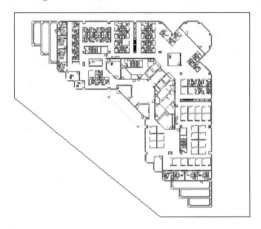

Converting an Object to a Viewport

- The **Converting Object** command is used to convert an existing object to a viewport.
- First, you need to draw the object that will be converted to a viewport, such as a circle, polyline, ellipse, etc.
- To start the **Converting Object** command, make sure you are in the **View** tab on the **Ribbon**, and, using the **Viewports** panel, click the **Create from Object** button.

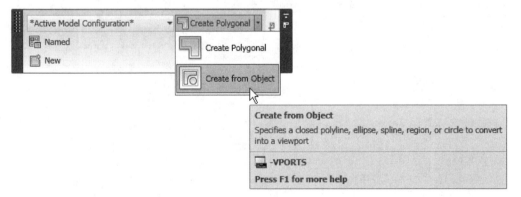

- The following prompt will appear:

```
Specify corner of viewport or
[ON/OFF/Fit/Shadeplot/Lock/Object/Polygonal/
Restore/LAyer/2/3/4] <Fit>: _o
Select object to clip viewport:
```

- See the following illustration:

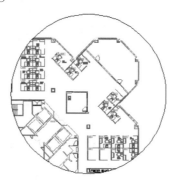

Clipping an Existing Viewport

- If you have a rectangular viewport, you can change it to an irregular shape by clipping it.
- To start the **Viewport Clip** command, make sure you are in the **View** tab on the **Ribbon**, and, using the **Viewports** panel, click the **Clip** button.

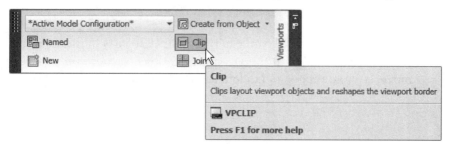

- The following prompt will appear:

```
Select viewport to clip:
Select clipping object or [Polygonal] <Polygonal>:
Specify start point:
Specify next point or [Arc/Length/Undo]:
Specify next point or [Arc/Close/Length/Undo]:
```

- First, select the existing viewport. You can draw a polyline or any irregular shape using the **Polygonal** option, which is identical to the **Polygonal viewport**.

- See the following illustration:

10.9 MODEL SPACE AND PAPER SPACE MODES IN LAYOUTS

- In a layout, you deal with the viewports in two modes:
  - **Paper Space** mode
  - **Model Space** mode

Paper Space Mode

- The **Paper Space** mode is the default mode in any layout.
- In the **Status Bar**, you will see the following:

- As previously discussed, you can place the viewports in this mode.
- Also, you can deal with the viewports as objects; therefore, you can copy, move, stretch, rotate, and delete them. For example:

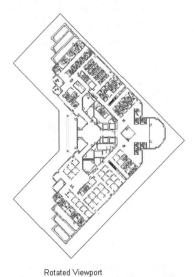

Rotated Viewport

Model Space Mode

- In **Model Space** mode you will get inside the viewport.
- You can zoom in, zoom out, and pan while you are in this mode.
- Also, you can scale each viewport.
- Furthermore, you can change the status of the layers for the current viewports.
- There are two ways to enter this mode:
  - Double-click inside the desired viewport.
  - Click the **Paper** button on the **Status Bar** and it will switch to **Model** as shown:

- In order to switch from **Model Space** mode to **Paper Space** mode, either double-click outside any viewport or click the **Model** button on the **Status Bar**.

10.10 MODIFYING, SCALING, AND MAXIMIZING VIEWPORTS

- Each viewport can be modified, scaled, or maximized to fill the whole screen.

Modifying

- Each viewport is considered an object. It can be copied, moved, scaled, rotated, and deleted. You have to select each viewport from its border in order to select it.
- You can select viewports first, and then issue the modifying command. Conversely, you can issue the command and then select the desired viewports.

Scaling

- Each viewport should be scaled relative to the **Model Space** units.
  - Double-click inside the desired viewport. You will switch to the **Model Space** mode for this viewport.
  - Look at the right side of the **Status Bar**, you will see the following:

- Click the pop-up list that contains the scales. You will see something like the following:

```
Scale to fit
1:1
1:2
1:4
1:5
1:8
1:10
1:16
1:20
1:30
1:40
1:50
1:100
2:1
4:1
8:1
10:1
100:1
1/128" = 1'-0"
1/64" = 1'-0"
1/32" = 1'-0"
1/16" = 1'-0"
3/32" = 1'-0"
1/8" = 1'-0"
3/16" = 1'-0"
1/4" = 1'-0"
3/8" = 1'-0"
1/2" = 1'-0"
3/4" = 1'-0"
1" = 1'-0"
1-1/2" = 1'-0"
3" = 1'-0"
6" = 1'-0"
1'-0" = 1'-0"
Custom...
✔ Hide Xref scales
```

- Select the suitable scale to be used in the viewport.
- If you did not find the desired scale, select the **Custom** option. You will see the following dialog box:

- Click the **Add** button to add a new scale. You will see the following dialog box:

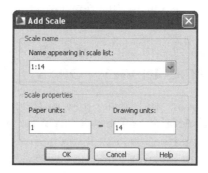

- Type in the desired scale and click **OK** twice.
- After you set the scale, you can use the **Pan** command. However, if you want to use the **Zoom** command, the scale value will be invalid and you will have to repeat the procedure of setting the scale again.
- In order to avoid this problem, you can lock the display of the viewport by clicking the golden opened lock in the **Status Bar** (you have to be inside the viewport in order for this to work). The golden lock will change to blue and it will be locked.

- There are two possible results once you have scaled a viewpoint:
  - The scale is perfect for the area of the viewport. Leave it as is.
  - The scale is either too small or too big. You can change the scale or change the area of the viewport.

Maximizing

- After placing and scaling your viewports, there will be small ones and big ones.
- For small ones, you can maximize the area of the viewport to be as large as your screen. You can do all of your work and then return it to the original size.
- Using the **Status Bar**, click the **Maximize Viewport** button:

- The same button will change to **Minimize Viewport** in order to restore the original size of the viewport.
- NOTE ▸ Another way of maximizing the viewport is to double-click the <u>border</u> of the viewport.

10.11 FREEZING LAYERS IN VIEWPORTS

- Earlier in this book we learned how to freeze a layer. This tool will be effective in both **Model Space** and **Layouts**.
- In **Layouts**, if you freeze a layer it will be frozen in all viewports. You may want to freeze certain layer(s) in one of the viewports and not in others. To do so, you have to freeze the layer in the current viewport.
- Perform the following tasks:
  - Make the desired viewport current by double-clicking inside it.
  - Make sure you are in the **Home** tab on the **Ribbon**, and, using the **Layers** panel, click the **Freeze or thaw in current viewport** icon for the desired layer. See the following image:

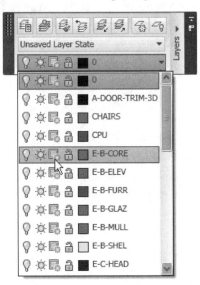

10.12 LAYER OVERRIDE IN VIEWPORTS

- **Color**, **Linetype**, **Lineweight**, and **Plot Style** are the same for all layers in all viewports.
- You can assign different colors, linetypes, lineweights, or plot styles for each layer in each viewport. This is called **Layer Override**.

- Perform the following steps:
  - Double-click inside the desired viewport.
  - Start the **Layer Properties Manager**.
  - Under **all/any** of **VP Color**, **VP Linetype**, **VP Lineweight**, or **VP Plot Style**, make the desired changes.
  - You will see that changes only take place in the current viewport.
  - See the following image:

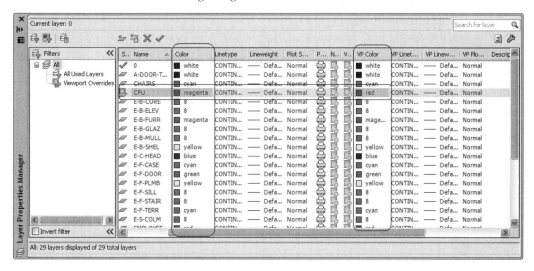

- You can see that the **CPU** layer has a magenta normal color and a red override color in the current viewport (this applies in **Model Space** and all other viewports).
- Also, note that the row containing the **CPU** layer is shaded with a different color.

INSERTING AND SCALING VIEWPORTS (METRIC)

Workshop 20-A

1. Start AutoCAD 2010.
2. Open the file *Workshop_20.dwg*.
3. Select **ISO A1 Layout**.
4. Make the **Viewports** layer current.
5. Turn **OSNAP** off.
6. Select the **View** tab from the **Ribbon**, and, using the **Viewports** panel, click the **New** button. Select the arrangement **Three: Left**, and set the **Viewport spacing** = 5.

7. Click **OK** and specify two opposite corners so the three viewports fill the empty space.

8. Select the big viewport at the left and set the scale = 1:50, the upper viewport scale = 1:20, and the lower viewport scale to be 1:30.

9. Double-click outside the viewports to move to the **Paper** mode.

10. Freeze the **Dimension** layer and thaw **Furniture**, **Hatch**, and **Text**.

11. Make the big left viewport the current viewport, and freeze the layers **Furniture**, **Hatch**, and **Text**.

12. Make the upper viewport current and pan to the Master Bedroom (do not use the zooming options). Make the lower viewport current and pan to the Living Room.

13. Double-click outside the viewports to move to the **Paper** mode.

14. Lock the view in the three viewports.

15. The drawing should look like the following:

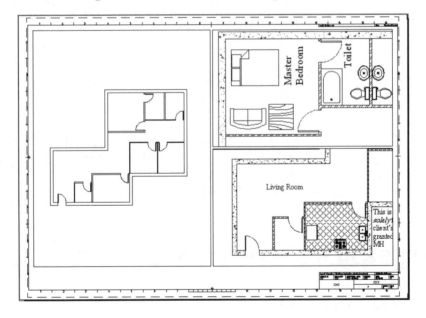

16. Save the file and close it.

INSERTING AND SCALING VIEWPORTS (IMPERIAL)

Workshop 20-B

1. Start AutoCAD 2010.

2. Open the file *Workshop_20.dwg*.

3. Select **D-Sized Layout**.

4. Make the **Viewports** layer current.

5. Turn **OSNAP** off.

6. Make sure you are in the **View** tab on the **Ribbon**, and, using the **Viewports** panel, click the **New** button. Select the arrangement **Three: Left**, and set the **Viewport spacing** = 0.35.

7. Click **OK** and specify two opposite corners so the three viewports fill the empty space.

8. Select the big viewport at the left and set the scale to be ¼" = 1', and the upper and lower viewports scale to be ½" = 1'.

9. Double-click outside the viewports to move to the **Paper** mode.

10. Freeze the layer **Dimension** and thaw **Furniture**, **Hatch**, and **Text**.

11. Make the big left viewport the current viewport and freeze the layers **Furniture**, **Hatch**, and **Text**.

12. Make the upper viewport current and pan to the Master Bedroom (do not use the zooming options). Make the lower viewport current and pan to the Living Room.

13. Double-click outside the viewports to move to the **Paper** mode.

14. Lock the view in the three viewports.

15. The drawing should look like the following:

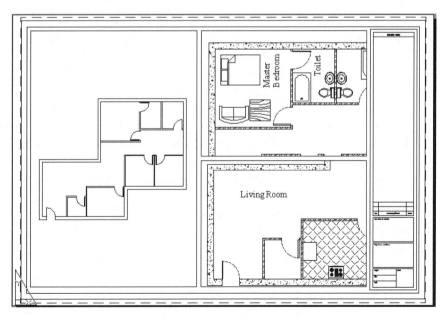

16. Save the file and close it.

10.13 AN INTRODUCTION TO PLOT STYLE TABLES

- There are many colors available in AutoCAD, but, will these colors print?
- There are two possibilities:
  - You will use the same colors in both the softcopy and the hardcopy of the drawing.
  - You will assign a different color in the hardcopy for each color in the softcopy.
- To translate the colors between softcopy and hardcopy, we need to create a **Plot Style**.
- There are two types of **Plot Styles**:
  - **Color-Dependent Plot Style Table**
  - **Named Plot Style Table**

10.14 THE COLOR-DEPENDENT PLOT STYLE TABLE

- This method is almost the same method used prior to AutoCAD 2000; it depends on the colors used in the drawing file.
- Each color used in the drawing file will be printed with a color chosen by the user. Also, users can set the lineweight, linetype, etc., for each color.
- This method is limited because there are only 255 colors to use.
- Also, if there are two layers with the same color, you will be forced to use the same output color, with the same lineweight, linetype, etc.
- Each time you create a **Color-Dependent Plot Style Table**, AutoCAD will ask you to name a file with the extension *.ctb*.
- You can create **Plot Style Tables** from outside AutoCAD (using the **Windows Control Panel**) or from inside AutoCAD using the **Wizards**. This will only initiate the command, but the command is the same either way.
- From outside AutoCAD, start the **Windows Control Panel** and double-click the **Autodesk Plot Style Manager** icon. Since this command is not available on the **Ribbon**, you can type **stylesmanager** in the **Command Window**.
- You will see the following window:

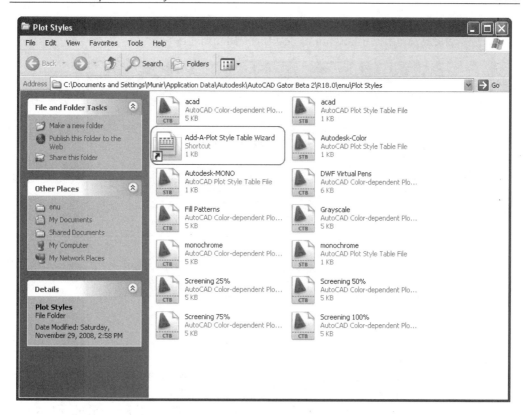

- Double-click **Add-A-Plot Style Table Wizard**.
- The following dialog box will appear:

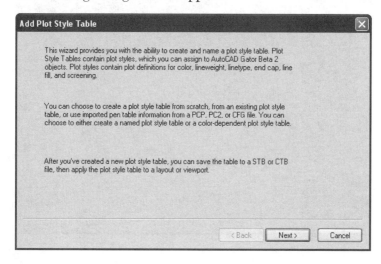

- In this dialog box, AutoCAD explains the next few steps in this process. Click **Next** and the following dialog box will appear:

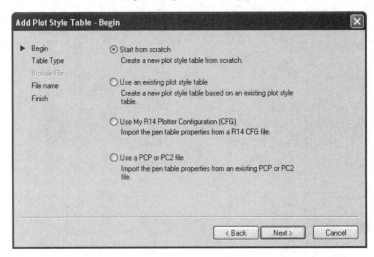

- You have four choices to select from:
  - Start creating your style from scratch.
  - Use an existing plot style.
  - Import the *AutoCAD R14 CFG* file and create a plot style from it.
  - Import the *PCP* or *PC2* file and create a plot style from it.
- Select **Start from scratch** and click **Next**. The following dialog box will appear:

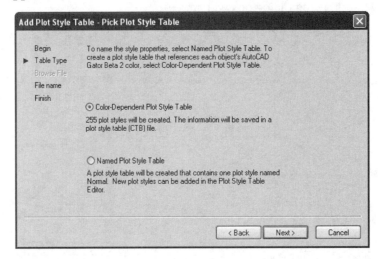

- Select **Color-Dependent Plot Style Table** and click **Next**.
- The following dialog box will appear:

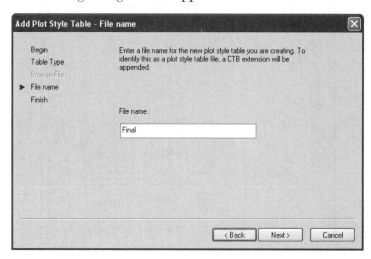

- Type in the name of the plot style and click **Next**. The following will appear:

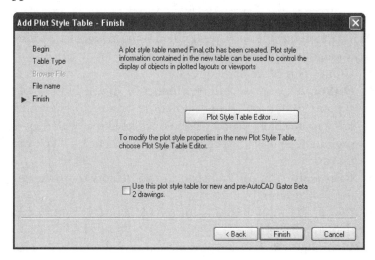

- You can use this plot style table for new and pre-AutoCAD 2010 drawings. Click the **Plot Style Table Editor** button and you will see the following:

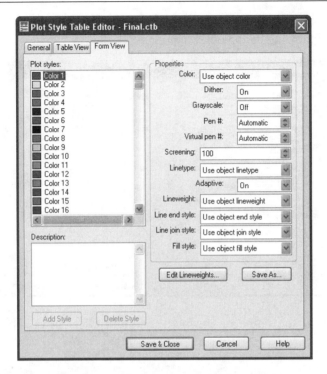

- At the left, select the color you used in your drawing file. At the right, change any or all of the following settings.
    - **Color**: This is the hardcopy color.
    - **Dither**: This option will be dimmed if your printer or plotter does not support dithering. Dither allows the printer to give the impression of using more colors than the limited 255 colors provided by AutoCAD. It is preferable to leave this option off. It should be on if you want **Screening** to work.
    - **Grayscale**: You can translate the 255 colors to grayscale grades (good for laser printers).
    - **Pen #**: This option is only for the old types of plotters—pen plotters—that are obsolete now.
    - **Virtual pen #**: This option is for non-pen plotters to simulate pen plotters by assigning a virtual pen to each color. It is preferable to leave this setting on **Automatic**.
    - **Screening**: This is good for trial printing. If you set numbers less than 100, it will reduce the intensity of the shading and fill hatches. You should turn **Dither** on so **Screening** will be effective.
    - **Linetype**: You can use the object's linetype or you can set a different linetype for each color.

- **Adaptive**: Used to change the linetype scale to fit the current line length so it will start with a segment and end with a segment instead of a space. Turn this option off if the linetype scale is important to the drawing.
- **Lineweight**: Sets the lineweight for the color selected. You can choose from a list of lineweights.
- **Line end style**: Used to specify the end style for lines. The available end styles are: **Butt**, **Square**, **Round**, and **Diamond**.
- **Line join style**: Used to specify the line join (the connection between two lines) style. The available styles are: **Miter**, **Bevel**, **Round**, and **Diamond**.
- **Fill style**: Used to set the fill style for the area filled in the drawing, which is good for trial printing.

■ Click **Save & Close** and then click **Finish**.

■ To link **Color-Dependent Plot Style** to a layout, perform the following steps:

- Go to the desired layout and start the **Page Setup Manager**.
- At the upper right section of the dialog box, change the **Plot style table (pen assignments)** setting to the desired *.ctb* file:

- Click the **Display plot styles** checkbox.

■ You can assign one *.ctb* file for each layout.

■ In order to see the lineweight of the objects, you must click on the **Show/ Hide Lineweight** button on the **Status Bar**.

10.15 THE NAMED PLOT STYLE TABLE

■ This is a new method introduced for the first time in AutoCAD 2000; it is not color-dependent.

■ You will create a **Plot Style** and give it a name. Each plot style will include different tables within it, which you will link with layers later on.

■ You can have two layers with the same color, but they will be printed with different colors, linetypes, and lineweights.

- The **Named Plot Style Table** has the file extension *.stb*.
- The creation procedure of the **Named Plot Style** is identical to that of the **Color-Dependent Plot Style**, except the last step, which uses the **Plot Style Table Editor** button.
- From outside AutoCAD, start the **Windows Control Panel** and double-click the **Autodesk Plot Style Manager** icon. Since this command is not available on the **Ribbon**, you can type **stylesmanager** in the **Command Window**.
- Double-click **Add-A-Plot Style Table Wizard**.
- Go through the dialog boxes until you reach the **Plot Style Table Editor** button. Click it and you will see the dialog box that follows.
- After you click the **Add Style** button, you will see the **Plot Style Table Editor** for the **Named Plot Style**:

- As you can see, you can change the **Name**, **Description**, or **Color**. The rest is identical to the **Color-Dependent Plot Style Table**. To change any of the elements listed:
  - Type in the **Name** of the style.
  - Type in any **Description** for this style.
  - Specify the **Color** that you will use in the hardcopy.
- You can add as many styles as you wish in the same **Named Plot Style**.
- Click **Save & Close** and then click **Finish**.
- In order to link a **Named Plot Style Table** with a drawing:

- You must first convert one of the *.ctb* files to a *.stb* file. Type **convertctb** in the **Command Window**. A dialog box with all the *.ctb* files will appear. Select one of them, keeping the same name or giving a new name, then click **OK**. The following dialog box will appear:

- Convert the drawing from **Color-Dependent Plot Style** to **Named Plot Style**. Type **convertpstyles** in the **Command Window**. The following warning message will appear:

- Click **OK** and the following dialog box will appear:

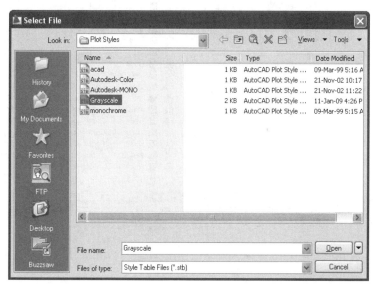

- Select the **Named Plot Style Table** you just converted and click **Open**. The following message will appear in the Command Window:

```
Drawing converted from Color Dependent mode to
Named plot style mode.
```

- Because you will use the **Named Plot Style Table** with layers, the **Model Space** and all layouts will be assigned the same *.stb* file.
- Go to the desired layout and start the **Page Setup Manager**. In the upper right-hand part of the dialog box, change the **Plot style table (pen assignments)** setting to the desired *.stb* file. Click the **Display plot styles** checkbox and end the **Page Setup Manager** command:

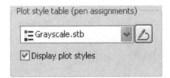

- Go to the **Layer Properties Manager** and search for the desired layer under the **Plot Style** column:

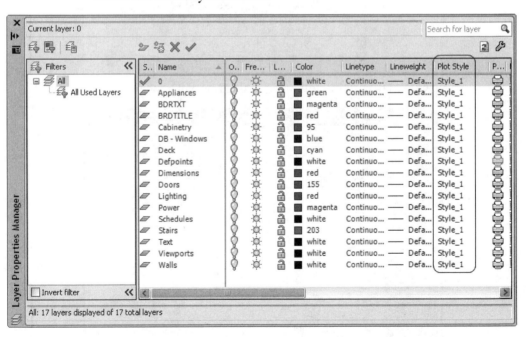

- Click the name of the current style. The following dialog box will appear:

- Select the desired plot style to be linked to the selected layer. When you are finished, click **OK**.

PLOT STYLE TABLES

 Exercise 40

1. Start AutoCAD 2010.
2. Open the file *Exercise_40.dwg*.
3. Click **Layout1**.
4. Start a new **Plot Style Table** and choose **Color-Dependant**. Call this plot style **Mechanical_BW** and make the following changes:

Drawing Color	Plotter Color	Linetype	Lineweight
Color 2	Black	Dashdot	0.30
Color 3	Black	Solid	0.70
Color 4	Black	Solid	0.50
Color 6	Black	Solid	0.50

5. Go to the **Page Setup Manager** and select **Plot style table** to be **Mechanical_BW**. Turn on **Display plot styles**.

6. Click the **Show/Hide Lineweight** button to see the effect of the lineweight.
7. Save the file as *Exercise_40_1.dwg*.
8. Type **convertctb** in the **Command Window** and convert **Mechanical_BW** from a *.ctb* to a *.stb* file.
9. Type **convertpstyles** in the **Command Window** to convert the whole drawing to accept **Named Plot Styles**. Select **Mechanical_BW** when you are asked to select a *.stb* file.
10. Start a new **Plot Style Table** and choose **Named Plot Style**. Call this plot style **Design_Process** and make the following changes:

Style	Description	Color	Linetype	Lineweight
Finished	Design is Final	Black	Solid	0.7
Incomplete	Incomplete Design	Green	Dashed	0.3

11. Go to the **Page Setup Manager** and select **Plot Style Table** to be **Design_Process**. Turn on **Display plot styles**.
12. Start the **Layer Manager** and set the plot style for layer **Base** to be **Finished**, and layers **Shaft** and **Body** to be **Incomplete**.
13. Click the **Show/Hide Lineweight** button to see the effect of the lineweight.
14. Issue the **Regenall** command if things do not appear correctly.
15. Save the file as *Exercise_40_2.dwg*.

10.16 THE PLOT COMMAND

- The final step in this process is to issue the **Plot** command, which will send your layout to the printer or plotter.
- As a first step, go to the desired layout you want to plot.
- To issue this command, make sure you are in the **Output** tab on the **Ribbon**, and, using the **Plot** panel, click the icon **Plot**.

- The following dialog box will appear:

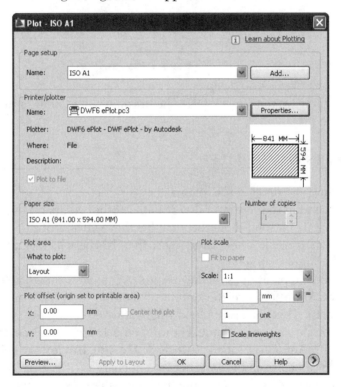

- As you can see, all of the settings are identical to those in **Page setup**.
- If you change any of these settings, AutoCAD will detach the **Page setup** from the current layout.
- Click the **Apply to Layout** button if you want this plot dialog box saved with this layout for future use.

- Click the **Preview** button in order to see the final printed drawing on the screen before the real printout. You can decide if your choices of plot styles and other settings are correct or not.
- You can preview your drawing from outside this dialog box. Make sure that you are in **Output** tab on the **Ribbon**, and, using the **Plot** panel, click the **Preview** button.

- After you are done, click **OK**. The drawing will be sent to the printer.

10.17 WHAT IS A DWF FILE?

- Assume one or all of the following:
  - You want to share your design with another company, but you are fearful that if you send them the *.dwg* file they will alter it.
  - Your *.dwg* file is very large (more than 1 MB), which may not be accepted by your email server.
  - The recipient does not have AutoCAD to view the *.dwg* file.
- AutoCAD offers you the option of plotting to a DWF file (<u>D</u>esign <u>W</u>eb <u>F</u>ormat). This file has the following features:
  - You do not need AutoCAD to open a DWF file. Free software comes with AutoCAD called **Autodesk Design Review**, which you can also download from the Internet free of charge.
  - You can view the file, zoom, pan, measure, markup, and print it.
  - The size is small so you can send it through email.
  - The recipient cannot modify it.

10.18 WHAT IS A DWFx FILE?

- A DWFx file was introduced by both Autodesk®, Inc., and Microsoft®.
- It will replace the DWF as the next generation file.

- If you are using Windows Vista, you will be able to view a DWFx file without any additional viewer.
- DWFx can be viewed using Windows Internet Explorer.

10.19 EXPORTING DWF, DWFx, AND PDF FILES

- You can export DWF, DWFx, and PDF files using AutoCAD 2010.
- To start exporting, make sure you are in the **Output** tab on the **Ribbon**, and, using the **Export to DWF/PDF** panel, click any of the following three buttons:

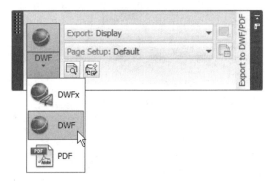

- The dialog box for the three types is identical:

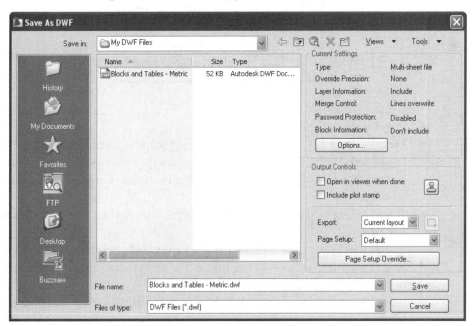

- Specify the hard disk, folder, and the name of the file.
- Read the **Current Settings** at the upper right-hand part of the dialog box:

- If these are the settings you want, go to the next step. If not, click the **Options** button and you will see the following dialog box:

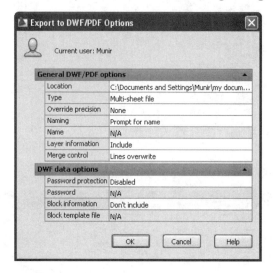

- Adjust the following settings:
  - Specify the location of the file.
  - Decide if the file will be **Single sheet** (current layout) or **Multi-sheet** (all layouts). While exporting, it will always produce a single layout that is the current layout. This option will be discussed along with the **Publish** command.
  - If you select a **Multi-sheet file**, determine whether or not to **Prompt for name**.
  - Select whether or not to include the **Layer information** in the file.
  - Select whether or not to include a **Password** for the DWF file. This option is not available for the PDF file.
  - Select whether to include the **Block information** (like attributes) in the file.

- Once you are done, click **OK**.
- Under the **Output Controls**:

- Adjust the following:
  - Select whether to open the file in the viewer when done or not.
  - Select whether to include a **plot stamp** or not.
  - Select what to export. If you are at a layout, **Current layout** will be selected automatically.
  - Select the **Page Setup**. AutoCAD will select the page setup included inside the layout. You can select any other page setups that exist in the drawing or you can create a temporary page setup for this plot only.
- When you are done, click the **Save** button.

10.20 THE PUBLISH COMMAND

- The **Publish** command will produce a DWF file containing multiple layouts from the current drawing and from other drawings.
- To issue the **Publish** command, make sure you are in the **Output** tab on the **Ribbon**, and, using the **Plot** panel, click the **Batch Plot** button:

- The following dialog box will appear:

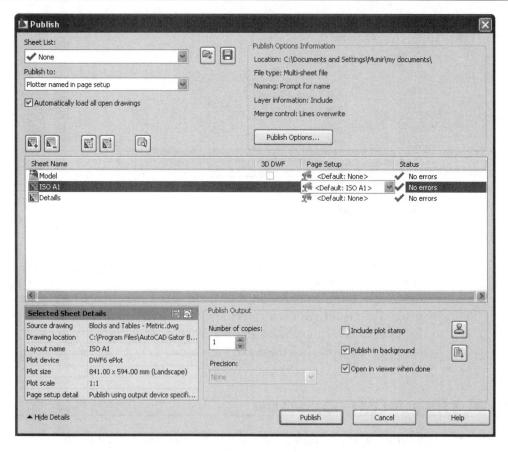

- You will see a list of the current file's **Model Space** and layouts.
- You can specify a previously saved **Sheet list** in the current drawing or you can:

  - Click the open folder icon to open a previously saved **Sheet list**.

  - Click the disk icon to save a **Sheet list** for future printing.

  - Select whether you want to use the printer/plotter defined in the layout or a DWF, DWFx, or PDF.
  - Select whether to load all open drawings automatically or not.
- Select one of the sheets and use the following buttons:

  - This button adds more sheets from other drawings. The **Select Drawings** dialog box will be shown to select the desired file.

  - This button removes one or more sheets from the list.

- This button moves the sheet up the list.

- This button moves the sheet down the list.

- Use this button to preview the selected sheet (only single sheet) as we did in **Print Preview**.

■ Click **Publish Options** and you will see the following dialog box:

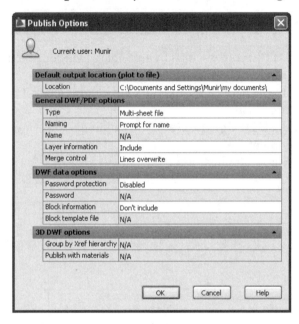

- This dialog box was discussed in the section on DWF, DWFx, and PDF exporting.
- **Multi-sheet file** means all sheets in the current sheet list.

■ Specify the number of copies.

■ To include a **Plot Stamp** in each sheet, check **Include plot stamp**.

■ Select whether you want to publish in the background or not.

■ Select whether to open the file in the viewer when done or not.

■ You can see more details about the selected sheet, such as **Plot device**, **Plot size**, **Plot scale**, etc.

■ Once you are done setting all of these, click the **Publish** button. AutoCAD will create the sheets one by one.

■ Check the right-hand side of **Status Bar**; you will see something like:

- When done, you will see the following message:

10.21 HOW TO VIEW DWF AND DWFx FILES

- AutoCAD 2010 comes with a free-of-charge viewer called **Autodesk Design Review** to view DWF and DWFx files.
- In order to open a DWF or DWFx file, double-click it and the software will open it immediately.
- In **Autodesk Design Review**, you can make some measurements and add some comments.
- See the following illustration:

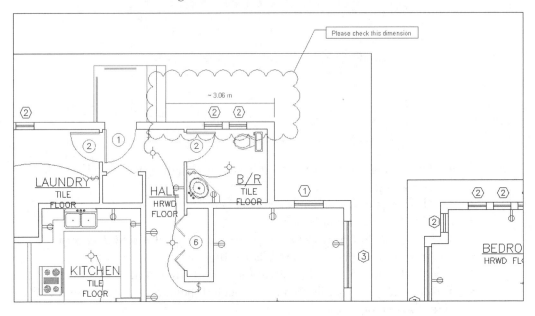

CREATING A MULTIPLE-SHEET DWF FILE (METRIC AND IMPERIAL)

  Workshops 21-A and 21-B

1. Start AutoCAD 2010.
2. Open the file *Workshop_21.dwg*.

3. Start the **Publish** command.

4. Select the **Model Space** sheet and remove it.

5. Add new sheets by selecting **Add sheets**. Browse for AutoCAD 2010\ Sample\Blocks and *Tables – Metric.dwg*.

6. Remove the **Model Space** sheet.

7. Make the **ISO A1** sheet the top sheet.

8. Select the **Publish to DWF** file.

9. Click the **Publish** button to create the file. It will ask you for the filename and place to save the file in; specify accordingly.

10. **Publish** will be done in the background. You can see this from the tray at the lower right-hand corner of the AutoCAD 2010 window.

11. After the background publishing, browse to the place you saved the file in and double-click it. **Autodesk Design Review** will open automatically and start to show you the contents of the DWF file.

CHAPTER REVIEW

1. What should you control in **Page Setup**?
   a. Paper size
   b. Which plotter to send to
   c. Viewports
   d. A and B

2. Layouts contain _____ and each can be assigned its own scale.

3. DWF files can be single sheet or multiple sheets.
   a. True
   b. False

4. You can choose whether or not to include the Layers in a DWF file.
   a. True
   b. False

5. The **Named Plot Style Table** file extension is:
   a. *filename.ctb*
   b. *filename.stb*
   c. *filename.sbt*
   d. *filename.bct*

6. If you assign a plot style to a layer in a **Named Plot Style Table**, you need to click the _____ button from the **Status bar** to see this lineweight in the layout.

CHAPTER REVIEW ANSWERS

1. d
2. Viewports
3. a
4. a
5. b
6. **Show/Hide Lineweight**

Appendix A

HOW TO CREATE A TEMPLATE FILE

In This Appendix

◊ Introduction
◊ Which Elements Are Included in a Template File?
◊ How to Create a Template File

A.1 INTRODUCTION

- Companies using AutoCAD® are always looking for better ways to:
  - Unify their work to a certain standard (homemade or international).
  - Speed up the process of producing a drawing.
- The answer to these two issues is to create a template file.
- Template files will reassure the decision makers in any company that all the premade settings for the drawings are already done in the templates. This will cut production time by at least 30%.
- Also, templates—which will be provided to all users in the company—will guarantee that these people will be using the same source; accordingly, no personal initiative will be allowed and the results will be uniform.
- Template files are *.dwt*.

A.2 WHICH ELEMENTS ARE INCLUDED IN A TEMPLATE FILE?

- These are the elements included in a template file:
  - **Drawing units**
  - **Drawing limits**
  - **Grid** and **Snap** settings
  - **Layers**
  - **Linetypes**
  - **Text Styles**
  - **Dimension Styles**
  - **Table Styles**

- **Layouts** (including **Border blocks** and **Viewports**)
- **Page Setups**
- **Plot Style tables**

- There is no need to include blocks in the template file. Instead, store them in files with each category in a separate file, such as Architectural, Civil, Mechanical, etc.).
- You cannot save **Tool Palettes** inside template files because **Tool Palettes** will be available for all files in a single computer.

A.3 HOW TO CREATE A TEMPLATE FILE

- Start AutoCAD 2010.
- Complete the paperwork to prepare the settings required. This step may involve consultation with other people who operate AutoCAD in the same company.
- Create a new file using the simplest template file, *acad.dwt*.
- The new file will contain the minimum drawing requirements.
- Build all of the necessary elements inside this file.
- Once you are done, select **Save As** and **AutoCAD Drawing Template** from the application menu.

■ The following dialog box will appear:

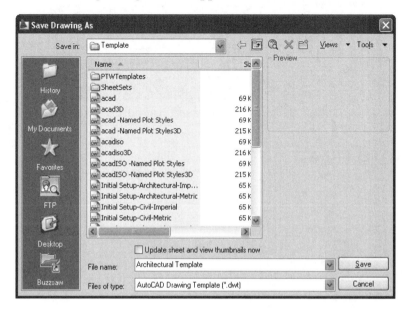

■ Type in the template file name.
■ By default, you can save your file in the template folder that comes with the software.
■ Alternately, you can create a new folder to accommodate all of your template files.
■ It is highly recommended that you store your files in a different folder away from the AutoCAD folders.
■ You can create as many templates as you wish.
■ If you want to edit an existing template, perform the following tasks:
  • Select **Open/Drawing** from the application menu:

- Select **Drawing Template** (**.dwt*) from **Files of type**:

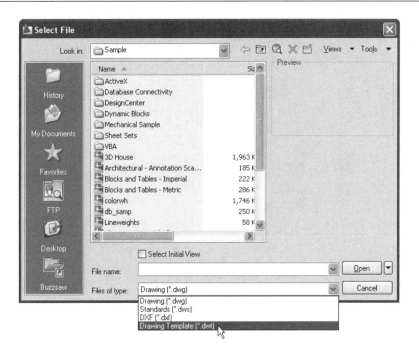

- Open the desired template and make the desired changes.
- Save it under the same name or use a new name.

B Appendix INQUIRY COMMANDS

In This Appendix
◇ Introduction
◇ The **Distance** Command
◇ The **Radius** Command
◇ The **Angle** Command
◇ The **Area** Command

B.1 INTRODUCTION

- Inquiry commands are used to:
  - Measure a distance between two points.
  - Measure the radius of a circle or an arc.
  - Measure an angle.
  - Calculate the area between points or of an object.
- AutoCAD® provides a single command that includes all of these functions; this command is the **MEASUREGEOM** command.
- To reach this command, make sure you are in the **Home** tab on the **Ribbon**, and select the **Utilities** panel.

B.2 THE DISTANCE COMMAND

- The **Distance** command is used to measure the distance between two points.
- Make sure you are in the **Home** tab on the **Ribbon**, and, selecting the **Utilities** panel, click the **Distance** button:

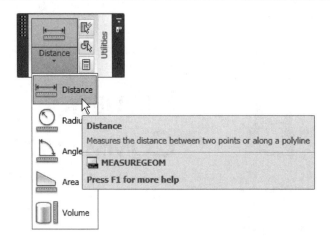

- AutoCAD will display the following prompt:

```
Specify first point: (Specify first point)
Specify second point: (Specify Second point)
```

- Click on the two points desired. AutoCAD will display something like:

```
Distance = 10.0000,  Angle in XY Plane = 0,  Angle from XY
Plane = 0
Delta X = 10.0000,  Delta Y = 0.0000,   Delta Z = 0.0000
```

B.3 THE RADIUS COMMAND

- The **Radius** command is used to measure the radius of a circle or an arc.
- Make sure you are in the **Home** tab on the **Ribbon**, and, selecting the **Utilities** panel, click the **Radius** button:

- AutoCAD will display the following prompt:

```
Select arc or circle: (Select the desired arc or circle)
```

- Select the desired arc or circle. AutoCAD will display something like:

```
Radius = 6.6294
Diameter = 13.2588
```

B.4 THE ANGLE COMMAND

- The **Angle** command is used to measure the angle between two lines included in an arc, between a circle's center and two points, or between a selected vertex and two points.
- Make sure you are in the **Home** tab on the **Ribbon**, and, selecting the **Utilities** panel, click the **Angle** button:

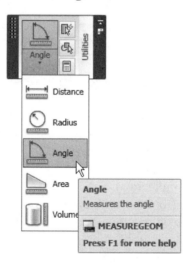

- AutoCAD will display the following prompt:

```
Select arc, circle, line, or <Specify vertex>:
```

- These are identical to the requirements of the **Angular dimension**.
- Select the desired arc or circle. AutoCAD will display something like:

```
Angle = 120°
```

B.5 THE AREA COMMAND

- The **Area** command is used to calculate the area between points or the area of an object.
- Make sure you are in the **Home** tab on the **Ribbon**, and, selecting the **Utilities** panel, click the **Area** button:

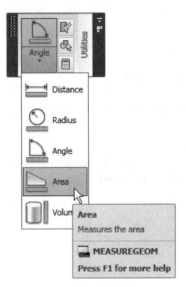

- You can calculate the area for:
  - Points (assuming there are lines connecting them)
  - Objects such as a circle or a polyline (closed or open)
- You can calculate two types of areas:
  - Simple area (single area)
  - Complex area (to determine the net area)
- If you start the **Area** command and specify the points or select the object, AutoCAD will calculate the simple area.
- To calculate the complex area, you must start with either **Add** or **Subtract**.
- Click the **Area** button.
- AutoCAD will display the following prompt:

```
Specify first corner point or [Object/Add
area/Subtract area/eXit] <Object>:
```

Specify the First Corner

- A simple area consists of points connected by lines or arcs. Specify the first point and AutoCAD will prompt:

```
Specify next point or [Arc/Length/Undo]:
Specify next point or [Arc/Length/Undo]:
Specify next point or [Arc/Length/Undo/Total] <Total>:
```
(After the third point, you can ask for Total value of area measured)
```
Specify next point or [Arc/Length/Undo/Total] <Total>:
```

- Continue specifying points until you press [Enter] to get the total value of the measured area. The following message will appear:

```
Area = 33.3750, Perimeter = 23.6264
```

Object

- To calculate the area by selecting an object, such as a circle or polyline, press [Enter] as the **Object** option is the default option. You can also type **O** or right-click and select **Object**. AutoCAD will prompt:

```
Select objects:
```

- Once you select the desired object, AutoCAD will report the following (in this example the object is a circle):

```
Area = 28.2743, Circumference = 18.8496
```

Add Area/Subtract Area

- You need the **Add area** mode or **Subtract area** mode in order to calculate a complex area—which are areas inside areas—in order to get the net area.
- Start with either one of these two modes and AutoCAD will assume that you are starting with **Area** = 0.00. Hence, you will add the outer area and then subtract the inner areas, or you can subtract the inner areas and then add the outer areas.
- Assume you started with the **Add area** mode. AutoCAD will prompt you to:

```
Specify first corner point or [Object/Subtract
area/eXit]:
```

- You can specify area(s) using either points or an object. When you are done, switch to **Subtract area** mode, and so on.
- While you are adding and subtracting, AutoCAD will give you the current value of the area until the last area has been added/subtracted.
- Once you are done, press [Enter] twice and AutoCAD will report the final value of the area.

- The following are possible prompts for **Add area/Subtract area:**

```
Specify first corner point or [Object/Add
area/Subtract area/eXit] <Object>: A
Specify first corner point or [Object/Subtract
area/eXit]: O
(ADD mode) Select objects:

Area = 44.0000, Perimeter = 30.0000
Total area = 44.0000
(ADD mode) Select objects:
Area = 44.0000, Perimeter = 30.0000
Total area = 44.0000


Specify first corner point or [Object/Subtract
area/eXit]: S
Specify first corner point or [Object/Add area/eXit]:
O
(SUBTRACT mode) Select objects:
Area = 3.1416, Circumference = 6.2832
Total area = 40.8584
(SUBTRACT mode) Select objects:


Specify first corner point or [Object/Add area/eXit]:


Total area = 40.8584
```

- You will see something like the following illustration:

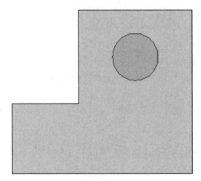

INDEX